THE EVERYTHING® JUMBO BOOK OF
LARGE-PRINT BIBLE WORD SEARCHES

160 inspiring puzzles in large print

Charles Timmerman
Founder of Funster.com

Adams Media
New York London Toronto Sydney New Delhi

Adams Media
An Imprint of Simon & Schuster, Inc.
57 Littlefield Street
Avon, Massachusetts 02322

An Everything® Series Book. Everything® and everything.com® are registered trademarks of Simon & Schuster, Inc.

First Adams Media trade paperback edition June 2019

ADAMS MEDIA and colophon are trademarks of Simon & Schuster.

For information about special discounts for bulk purchases, please contact Simon & Schuster Special Sales at 1-866-506-1949 or business@simonandschuster.com.

The Simon & Schuster Speakers Bureau can bring authors to your live event. For more information or to book an event contact the Simon & Schuster Speakers Bureau at 1-866-248-3049 or visit our website at www.simonspeakers.com.

Interior design by Julia Jacintho

Manufactured in the United States of America

6 2023

ISBN 978-1-5072-1061-1

Contains material adapted from the following titles published by Adams Media, an Imprint of Simon & Schuster, Inc.: *The Everything® Large-Print Bible Word Search Book, Volume II* by Charles Timmerman, copyright © 2013, ISBN 978-1-4405-5930-3 and *The Everything® Large-Print Bible Word Search Book, Volume III* by Charles Timmerman, copyright © 2013, ISBN 978-1-4405-6452-9.

Contents

Contents

Puzzles

Our Many Sins

Habakkuk 1:12–16

O **Lord** my **God**, my **Holy One**, you who are eternal—**surely** you do not **plan** to **wipe** us **out**? O Lord, our **Rock**, you have sent these Babylonians to **correct** us, to **punish** us for our **many sins**. But you are **pure** and **cannot stand** the **sight** of **evil**. Will you **wink** at **their** treachery? Should you be **silent while** the **wicked swallow** up **people** more righteous than they? Are we only **fish** to be **caught** and **killed**? Are we only **sea** creatures that have no **leader**? **Must** we be **strung** up on their **hooks** and caught in their **nets** while they **rejoice** and **celebrate**? Then they will **worship** their nets and **burn** incense in front of them. "These nets are the gods who have **made** us rich!" they will **claim**. (NLT)

```
U I H F H U Q J B H M U S T
S D S T R U N G O F A A T S
Q W I C K E D O P L D C E B
B I N K C N K T L E E A N S
M N U V O S W A L L O W E C
G K P E R S U R E L Y P U T
O K I R R N C B L E R Q L H
P W H E E K R S I N S T S E
O U S D C A C T H O E I V I
K G R A T P U O W B F I T R
W W O E E O L D R O L D S M
J I W L J Y N A M T B N I L
A E P L D O G N N E R A G B
A H D E L L I K A U L T H E
I N T H G U A C B C Y S T E
B L P O Y S I L E N T A G A
```

Solution on Page 328

I Will Free You

Exodus 6:6–9

"Therefore, **say** to the **people** of **Israel**: 'I am the **LORD**. I will **free** you **from** **your** **oppression** and will **rescue** you from your slavery in **Egypt**. I will **redeem** you with a powerful **arm** and **great** **acts** of **judgment**. I will **claim** you as my **own** people, and I will be your **God**. Then you will know that I am the LORD your God who has freed you from your oppression in Egypt. I will **bring** you **into** the **land** I **swore** to **give** to **Abraham**, Isaac, and **Jacob**. I will give it to you as your **very** own **possession**. I am the LORD!'" So **Moses** **told** the people of Israel **what** the LORD had said, but they **refused** to **listen** **anymore**. They had **become** too discouraged by the **brutality** of **their** slavery. (NLT)

Solution on Page 328

```
Y D S L E T P L A S K S L R
D O G L A V Y R I E H T R V
V W U H E N I C B K A L C L
Y F W R J U D G M E N T L J
N Z Y J P J O A R O C K A E
L B A A A A E H G I T S O I U
O F S C R A B S B N L E M J
E O T O R V S R D I D B S E
R S W B M E U S L E A R S I
O S A N R T N J S P K I R T
M Z W P A E Y U L E R N V R
Y C P L T F F F R O M G E S
N O I S S E S S O P E D G N
A T I D R O L C J L E L Y A
Y L N U R E S C U E R O P Y
Z L D D U J Y D M D F T T T
```

Solution on Page 328

Servant and Master Are Equal

The Gospel of John 13:12–18

When he had washed **their** **feet** and put on his **outer** **garments** and **resumed** his **place**, he said to them, "Do you **understand** **what** I have done to you? You call me **Teacher** and **Lord**, and you are **right**, for so I am. If I then, **your** Lord and Teacher, have washed your feet, you also **ought** to **wash** **one** another's feet. For I have **given** you an **example**, that you also **should** do **just** as I have done to you. **Truly**, truly, I **say** to you, a **servant** is not **greater** than his **master**, **nor** is a messenger greater than the one who **sent** him. If you know these **things**, **blessed** are you if you do them. I am not **speaking** of **all** of you; I know **whom** I have chosen." (ESV)

Solution on Page 328

Puzzles

```
J B L L B G U H P Y B V B U
V P R L Q D A I L L O G N U
Q K D N A T S R E D N U O P
I T N A V R E S M I R N R U
J T A E T T S U K E E O H F
Z P N R H E B A L M N J L Y
F J U E D Q E P Y X M T N W
M L I S S P M W H A T Y S U
Y R B U S A X K S H O U L D
V Q R M X W R T A R F S F N
P G R E A T E R W E Q K U I
W L U D H R H W E T O W D G
N I A I D C C T H U S D Z P
T F N C H U A R G O A U Q F
T G I V E N E H Q I M R J Y
S F D R T J T H G I R A E I
```

Solution on Page 328

Deny Yourself

The Gospel of Matthew 16:24–28

Then **Jesus told** his **disciples**, "If **anyone would come after** me, let him **deny** himself and **take** up his **cross** and **follow** me. For whoever would save his **life** will lose it, but whoever loses his life for my sake will **find** it. For **what** will it **profit** a **man** if he **gains** the **whole world** and **forfeits** his soul? Or what **shall** a man **give** in **return** for his soul? For the **Son** of Man is **going** to come with his **angels** in the **glory** of his Father, and then he will **repay each** person **according** to what he has **done**. Truly, I **say** to you, there are some **standing here** who will not **taste death until** they **see** the Son of Man coming in his kingdom." (ESV)

```
Y F I W L R M S D T O L D I
E Z B S H E R E P A Y W L S
M G E V A A N E R D E P R N
Q I J K K Y T Q O G N I O G
W W F D G N D N F F O N W H
A A U O D H Z O I S Y R D R
G A I N S T A S T E N E E I
E N I E T G N I D N A T S S
D F I S X I E U G T F U C J
Q L I D E F L U H A A R Y Q
B F U L R M A N N L O N F J
U I O O A O O V Y S L T D E
O H F L W S C C S V W A M S
W C S E L P I C S I D K H U
X A E G L O R Y A N G E L S
E E V I G J W Q R Q U Y M Q
```

Solution on Page 328

Believe in the Light

The Gospel of John 12:32–36

"And I, when I am **lifted** up **from** the **earth**, will **draw** **all** **people** to myself." He said this to **show** by **what** **kind** of **death** he was **going** to **die**. So the **crowd** **answered** him, "We have heard from the **Law** that the **Christ** remains **forever**. How **can** you **say** that the Son of **Man** **must** be lifted up? Who is this Son of Man?" So **Jesus** said to them, "The **light** is among you for a **little** **while** longer. Walk while you have the light, **lest** **darkness** **overtake** you. The **one** who walks in the darkness does not **know** **where** he is going. While you have the light, **believe** in the light, that you may **become** sons of light." (ESV)

```
D O V N Y U C C G P H Q E M
N I E I T P T G H E N Q O F
L Z F Q C W H I L R R N J A
L J O X O P E D K A I E V Q
P E C H D A R K N E S S H H
L E S H R C M S M U S T T W
I A N T R W W N S X K A H T
Y N H O V E R T A K E D G H
I L W T R R D D O D R H I L
H D B E L I E V E F T E L E
N R D K M A N V S T L A W T
D A M F R O M G E P F B H W
X W C K X L C P O R Y I I W
Y R L I T T L E W I O Q L N
O W O N K Y P A B M N F E M
R A W D X K L A N T J G I R
```

Solution on Page 329

Jesus' Authority Is Challenged

The Gospel of Luke 20:1–8

One **day** **Jesus** was teaching the **people** in the **temple** courtyard and telling them the **Good** **News**. The **chief** **priests**, **scribes**, and **leaders** **came** up to him. They asked him, "**Tell** us, **what** **gives** you the **right** to do **these** **things**? Who **told** you that you **could** do this?" Jesus **answered** them, "I, too, have a question for you. Tell me, **did** **John**'s right to **baptize** **come** **from** **heaven** or from humans?" They **talked** **about** this among themselves. They said, "If we **say**, 'from heaven,' he will **ask**, 'Why didn't you **believe** him?' But if we say, 'from humans,' everyone will stone us to **death**. They're convinced that John was a prophet." So they answered that they didn't **know** who **gave** John the right to baptize. Jesus told them, "Then I won't tell you why I have the right to do these things." (GW)

```
R W Q R G U O D X D E A T H
J Z H I X P L M S U S E J B
F K J A R O H G T E M A C E
W O H H T U G C E P J C M L
A I T U V U F X L G O O D I
Z Y V E L P O E P H C T N E
F C T H G I R B I S W E N V
U W O N K B O I A H V L T E
U C H F S F Y N E A C L Z V
M O R S C R I B E S T I O A
J U X V T O E H B H T K H G
E L S H Y M L D I P J S K O
C D E R E W S N A Z Q A S D
J S V O W M G B D E K L A T
E L I L A S X T N I L Y Y O
P R G E T H G G X F D R C S
```

Solution on Page 329

Watch for Divisions

Romans 16:16–21

Greet **one** another with a **holy** **kiss**. **All** the churches of **Christ** greet you. I appeal to you, brothers, to **watch** **out** for **those** who **cause** divisions and **create** obstacles contrary to the doctrine that you have been **taught**; **avoid** them. For **such** persons do not **serve** our **Lord** Christ, but **their** **own** appetites, and by **smooth** talk and flattery they **deceive** the **hearts** of the **naive**. For your obedience is known to all, so that I **rejoice** **over** you, but I **want** you to be **wise** as to **what** is good and innocent as to what is **evil**. The **God** of **peace** will soon **crush** Satan **under** your **feet**. The **grace** of our Lord **Jesus** Christ be with you. **Timothy**, my fellow **worker**, greets you; so do **Lucius** and Jason and Sosipater, my **kinsmen**. (ESV)

```
N T T T Z G F I F U O H W T
P K H H W V E S B S W X B A
D H V L M A E S P W A T C H
G L G U K J T I U W N T B W
Z I O N Y R E K H I T H A I
Z N R D A P U S S S C G C N
E C A E P M N M U E S U A C
D U H R J A O N R S U A L E
E V I A N O T K C N P T Q G
C S E D T S I H T C T F S R
E Z E H I N M C R E A T E E
I T O R S R O U E L L K C E
V S H M V R T S L H R O A T
E C E E E E H A V O I D R R
E N E V I L Y O W L D O G D
T U O W N R F J O Y B D U X
```

Solution on Page 329

The Merchants Will Weep

Revelation 18:9–13

And the **kings** of the **world** who committed adultery with her and enjoyed her **great** **luxury** will mourn for her as they **see** the **smoke** rising **from** her charred remains. They will **stand** at a distance, terrified by her great torment. They will **cry** **out**, "How terrible, how terrible for you, O Babylon, you great **city**! In a single **moment** God's judgment **came** on you." The merchants of the world will **weep** and mourn for her, for there is no **one** **left** to **buy** **their** **goods**. She bought great quantities of **gold**, silver, **jewels**, and **pearls**; **fine** **linen**, purple, **silk**, and scarlet **cloth**; things **made** of fragrant thyine **wood**, **ivory** goods, and objects made of expensive wood; and bronze, iron, and **marble**. She **also** bought cinnamon, **spice**, incense, **myrrh**, frankincense, **wine**, **olive** **oil**, fine flour, **wheat**, **cattle**, **sheep**, horses, chariots, and bodies—that is, **human** slaves. (NLT)

```
U Y S U T T W I N E O I I W
Y L Z W N E H P R E W U P H
H V Z L E F T E F I N E K E
P C H P M A D E I R A O V A
B V L Z O Z C S G R K I R T
Y L Q O M A R B L E L S K W
V L C I T Y H S D O O G S S
F I X T Y H N R C Y P B R P
J N L G P I V O R Y U O N I
I E K I N G S U Y Y M G T C
P N W P R J X D A S M O K E
P J N E N U N K L I S L R P
U H A E L A X I S R D D D F
R T M H T S O O O B O Z H D
I A U S P U G B U S O W S S
C V H L T O O B T N W D O G
```

Solution on Page 329

Miracles and Healings

Acts 5:12–18

Now **many** **signs** and wonders were regularly **done** **among** the **people** by the **hands** of the apostles. And they were **all** together in Solomon's **Portico**. None of the **rest** **dared** **join** them, but the people **held** them in **high** **esteem**. And more than ever believers were **added** to the **Lord**, multitudes of **both** **men** and women, so that they **even** **carried** **out** the **sick** **into** the streets and **laid** them on **cots** and **mats**, that as **Peter** came by at **least** his **shadow** **might** fall on some of them. The people also gathered **from** the **towns** around Jerusalem, bringing the sick and **those** afflicted with unclean **spirits**, and they were all healed. But the high **priest** **rose** up, and all who were with him (that is, the **party** of the Sadducees), and **filled** with jealousy they arrested the apostles and put them in the **public** **prison**. (ESV)

```
M V Z I W R L A D N K L W X
G S S F S S T A S G A P P Z
C J O I N H S S I A D I C I
V X Y W C D A R E D E V E N
H T O B N K E D P R N D S T
Y T R A P T X E O F O P T O
N H H C E F O E R W D R A A
A O L P U P S G T E A I D F
M S N X L T P F I L L E D G
Y E E E E P I R C T S S E B
M S K E U T R Q O H S T D B
L N M B P A I I V J H A A E
X G L T C L T E S G M E E M
N I O O L L S T I O T O L L
C S R T U O O M N N N N M R D
D Y D W R C H G I H U G B F
```

Solution on Page 330

The Burning Bush

Exodus 3:1–6

Moses was taking **care** of the **sheep** of his father-in-law **Jethro**, the **priest** of **Midian**. As he **led** the sheep to the **far side** of the desert, he **came** to **Horeb**, the mountain of **God**. The Messenger of the **LORD appeared** to him **there** as **flames** of **fire** coming **out** of a **bush**. Moses **looked**, and although the bush was on fire, it was not **burning** up. So he thought, "Why isn't this bush burning up? I **must** go **over** there and **see** this **strange** sight." When the LORD **saw** that Moses had **come** over to see it, God called to him **from** the bush, "Moses, Moses!" Moses **answered**, "Here I am!" God said, "Don't come any closer! **Take off** your sandals because this **place where** you are **standing** is **holy** ground. I am the God of your ancestors." (GW)

```
E V V Z D J M G S H E E P O
O W E T Q N Z Z N N T L R R
K E T G Y G D W T I A D E S
S Z F K S H H C G C N E V K
L I K A H E S J E T H R O R
Y C Q P R I E S T T W A U J
M P F E D A M P Y U N E T B
X D W E G N A R T S O P S R
B J L U R O L P W T U P U M
S E Z D O T F E W A S A M C
V H M J D H R F C N Q E O E
D O S I D E N A I D I M R K
W L E U D R K E R I E A F A
R Y E H B E R O H N C C W T
U Q J O K I L D O G O E G N
D P K R F N V C U L I G O U
```

Solution on Page 330

Mount Sinai

Exodus 19:16–20

On the **morning** of the third **day** there were thunders and **lightnings** and a **thick** cloud on the mountain and a **very** loud **trumpet blast**, so that **all** the **people** in the **camp trembled**. Then **Moses** brought the people **out** of the camp to **meet God**, and they took **their stand** at the **foot** of the mountain. Now Mount **Sinai** was **wrapped** in **smoke because** the LORD had **descended** on it in **fire**. The smoke of it **went** up like the smoke of a **kiln**, and the **whole** mountain trembled greatly. And as the sound of the trumpet **grew** louder and louder, Moses **spoke**, and God **answered** him in thunder. The LORD came **down** on Mount Sinai, to the **top** of the mountain. And the LORD called Moses to the top of the mountain, and Moses went up. (ESV)

Solution on Page 330

```
B Y D D B P R K P P D Y R B
T U Z Q E K O M S O A Q G L
N S X O C S A O G T Y L X F
E J P D A C C S Z T S A L B
W L C G U G Y E A G H W Y C
E I N T S R N S N F P I F L
R R J O E A W I T D D U C H
G N I V U E N R N A E E H K
V F M F Z T M S A R N D Q G
N A B R H T O W W P O D E A
Z O K G O K R M H E P M O W
E A I A N I S U B O R E P O
X L Q L W T R E M B L E D T
X S I H O O E K O P S E D S
F K K D D O F V T H E I R Y
C S Z N Y F J P D U Z T A D
```

Solution on Page 330

The Trumpets

Revelation 8:6–10

Now the seven angels who had the seven trumpets **prepared** to **blow** them. The first **angel blew** his **trumpet**, and **there** followed hail and **fire**, **mixed** with blood, and these were **thrown upon** the **earth**. And a **third** of the earth was **burned** up, and a third of the **trees** were burned up, and **all** green **grass** was burned up. The second angel blew his trumpet, and something like a **great mountain**, burning with fire, was thrown **into** the **sea**, and a third of the sea became blood. A third of the **living creatures** in the sea **died**, and a third of the **ships** were **destroyed**. The third angel blew his trumpet, and a great **star fell from heaven**, **blazing** like a **torch**, and it fell on a third of the **rivers** and on the **springs** of water. (ESV)

```
J G J G Y C D E M O R F I A
E F W J R O T D U L E W K I
G O S J U K E P V L L S R A
R U E H X X O Y L B E A K V
A L I V I N G R E A T M Y K
S W A M G P E K G S Q T J H
S G N I R P S V N T N R J R
G M N W O R H T A D I E D W
E O J I E E B T H E R E O E
I R T V Z P S B Z Y H S H L
G W I N I A T N U O M U P B
O R I F I R L H T R A E U L
T R U M P E T B T T X R I O
F Q I K M D B A C S N Q U W
P T S S E R U T A E R C B F
H C R O T H I R D D Y A C T
```

Solution on Page 330

A Good Name

Proverbs 22:1–10

A **good** **name** is rather to be **chosen** than great riches, And **loving** favor rather than **silver** and gold. The **rich** and the **poor** **meet** together: **Jehovah** is the maker of them **all**. A **prudent** **man** **seeth** the **evil**, and **hideth** **himself**; But the **simple** **pass** on, and **suffer** for it. The reward of humility and the **fear** of Jehovah is riches, and **honor**, and **life**. Thorns and **snares** are in the **way** of the perverse: He that **keepeth** his **soul** shall be **far** from them. Train up a **child** in the way he **should** go, And **even** when he is **old** he will not **depart** from it. The rich **ruleth** **over** the poor; And the borrower is **servant** to the **lender**. He that **soweth** iniquity shall **reap** calamity; And the **rod** of his **wrath** shall fail. (ASV)

Solution on Page 330

```
H U Y P D O E K E E P E T H
A S L A S U F F E R A F A I
A W E E W Q R J U Z R V S M
K M C R G O O D W L O E N S
O P V H A F E A R H E L N E
Q L O V I N G F E T M S F L
R J I P T L S J H E A H R F
Q U O R N S D O C R N O C Q
F O G A A A A N H T E L U R R
R K M P V O O T X V W L O T
I E D D R S N E I L D D L E
C L D C E Y W D S I M P L E
H P I N S P R I R S G J A M
P W E V E N A H T E W O S D
H L I F E L T R S I V R L Z
Y P B N V O H C T L U O S F
```

Solution on Page 331

Sit in the Lowest Place

The Gospel of Luke 14:7–11

Now he **told** a **parable** to those who were **invited**, when he **noticed** how they chose the places of **honor**, saying to them, "When you are invited by **someone** to a **wedding feast**, do not **sit down** in a **place** of honor, **lest** someone more distinguished than you be invited by him, and he who invited you **both** will **come** and **say** to you, 'Give **your** place to this person,' and then you will **begin** with **shame** to **take** the **lowest** place. But when you are invited, go and sit in the lowest place, so that when your **host** comes he **may** say to you, 'Friend, **move** up higher.' Then you will be honored in the **presence** of **all** who sit at **table** with you. For **everyone** who exalts **himself** will be **humbled**, and he who humbles himself will be exalted." (ESV)

```
B I A T J V P X T X R M C L
I U G P B G E O T D W B K A
R X L O V Y G O D K K H Y C
J T W Y K N F N O T M L Y J
E L R D E P E Y I Y H G N H
S M V U V Y A M I D T A X K
D D Y E O S S R A W D O Q H
Q E E P M Y T C A T S E L S
F L C T R O B B L B F N W D
F S U I I E C A L P L O D P
B L U K T V S R L O W E S T
E V E R Y O N E T H L M H A
G K M S L D N I N B O O O B
I E A Q M W S I M C N S O L
N P H T O I O U W O E T T E
C S S D Z C H Y R K H E E S
```

Solution on Page 331

God Makes a Promise

Genesis 17:17–21

Immediately, **Abraham** **bowed** with his **face** **touching** the **ground**. He **laughed** as he **thought** to **himself**, "**Can** a **son** be **born** to a hundred-year-old **man**? Can **Sarah**, a ninety-year-old woman, have a child?" Then Abraham **said** to **God**, "Why not let Ishmael be my heir?" God **replied**, "No! **Your** **wife** Sarah will **give** you a son, and you will **name** him **Isaac**. I will make an everlasting **promise** to him and his descendants. I have **heard** your **request** **about** Ishmael. **Yes**, I will **bless** him, make him **fertile**, and **increase** the **number** of his descendants. He will be the **father** of 12 **princes**, and I will make him a **great** **nation**. But I will make my promise to Isaac. Sarah will give **birth** to him at this **time** **next** year." (GW)

34

```
Q F Y D B D Z R X D J A T T
F Y O U R N A E O B I S H C
E E M A N E A B I Z O A G X
M S E W F Z Q M O Q L R S G
I H I A M A G U N U E A N G
T F C M C R T N E A T H O I
E E D A O A P H T S T H S V
J T Q U B R A F E R T I L E
L D N G I R P S Z R H M O Z
V D Y N R D A D I F G S Q N
O M C I Q E E H I O U E X E
C E X H R H P S A D O L Q X
S A Q C G T Q L E M H F Y T
B B N U V R D W I Y T R O R
E I A O P I O B L E S S G W
P L J T J B G W N Z D L X G
```

Solution on Page 331

A Lamb for His Offering

Leviticus 3:3–7

And he shall **offer** of the **sacrifice** of the **peace** offering an offering **made** by **fire unto** the **LORD**; the **fat** that **covereth** the **inwards**, and **all** the fat that is **upon** the inwards, And the **two kidneys**, and the fat that is on them, **which** is by the **flanks**, and the **caul above** the **liver**, with the kidneys, it shall he **take away**. And Aaron's **sons** shall **burn** it on the altar upon the burnt sacrifice, which is upon the **wood** that is on the fire: it is an offering made by fire, of a **sweet savour** unto the LORD. And if his offering for a sacrifice of peace offering unto the LORD be of the **flock;** male or female, he shall offer it **without blemish**. If he offer a **lamb** for his offering, then shall he offer it **before** the LORD. (KJV)

```
S O D Y Q J Q K Y E P M G V
L Y J O U B U F H A O X L N
Z E E Y E E A T E E W S L T
R C E N U C E R C W H A H Z
P I F S D R A W N I I V O V
I F E D E I H E M U C Q V J
T I J V T A K E P A H Y U N
U R O S A V S O Y M D U O P
O C T Q F W N K N X R E H F
H A N D D R O L E E V E L Q
T S U E E X S R V O W O O D
I A I F O K O I B W C W W R
W V F M I F L A N K S A T T
Q O L O E R R H U I L H U N
B U C B L L E Y I L B M A L
N R U B W I B R R U G Z L F
```

Solution on Page 331

One Died for All

2 Corinthians 5:10–14

For we **must** **all** be made manifest **before** the judgment-seat of **Christ**; that **each** **one** **may** **receive** the **things** done in the **body**, **according** to what he **hath** done, **whether** it be good or **bad**. **Knowing** **therefore** the **fear** of the **Lord**, we **persuade** **men**, but we are made manifest **unto** **God**; and I **hope** that we are made manifest also in **your** consciences. We are not **again** commending **ourselves** unto you, but **speak** as **giving** you occasion of glorying on our behalf, that ye may have **wherewith** to **answer** them that glory in **appearance**, and not in **heart**. For whether we are **beside** ourselves, it is unto God; or whether we are of **sober** **mind**, it is unto you. For the **love** of Christ constraineth us; **because** we thus **judge**, that one **died** for all, therefore all died. (ASV)

```
T W L N Z M R G E Y U X J M
S H B P E R S U A D E A E H
U N I V F R L O V E I R C C
M E G N I W O N K G O S V S
N M C R G V R F N F Y I E O
G L T N A S D I E A C H W B
B N S I A N D B M R F H A E
E A I O U R S E L V E S U R
M Z R V O C A W K R R H N J
J L H C I D J E E A A V T U
G L C P N G V W P R E G O D
L A P I H I I I B L P F P D G
P R M T E T A B E C A U S E
A B A C H D Z G O N E W A P
W H E T H E R M A D I E D O
T R A E H I O R U O Y V Q H
```

Solution on Page 332

As for Me and My House

Joshua 24:15–17

"And if it is **evil** in your **eyes** to **serve** the **LORD**, **choose** this **day** **whom** you will serve, **whether** the gods your **fathers** served in the **region** **beyond** the **River**, or the gods of the Amorites in whose **land** you **dwell**. But as for me and my house, we will serve the LORD." Then the **people** **answered**, "Far be it **from** us that we should **forsake** the LORD to serve **other** gods, for it is the LORD our **God** who brought us and our fathers up from the land of **Egypt**, **out** of the house of **slavery**, and who **did** **those** **great** signs in our **sight** and preserved us in **all** the **way** that we **went**, and **among** all the peoples through whom we **passed**." (ESV)

Solution on Page 332

```
X D Q A E E G Y P T A E R G
Y R W H Q O I S A M S A X E
Z P A E O U K I S O W N S F
S X Z S L E F G S H E A T L
O E Q X Q L S H E W L N O J
A A Y A W P P T D L E S U P
Q P F E S O H T N W R W S Z
Y L Z O T E V I L E D E K Q
P Z E I R P Z A H I B R L M
L T V E O S Y T D T E E O K
L R H T S L A V E R Y D Q L
J T S E L F D K E S O O H C
O N R A M O N G E M N U X E
K V N C Y R I V E R D T F A
E D U W M O R F Q O P H H G
H T V Q N Y S W G C U X G L
```

Solution on Page 332

Paul and Silas in Prison

Acts 16:19–24

But when her **owners** **saw** that **their** **hope** of **gain** was **gone**, they **seized** **Paul** and **Silas** and **dragged** them **into** the marketplace **before** the **rulers**. And when they had **brought** them to the magistrates, they said, "These **men** are **Jews**, and they are disturbing our **city**. They **advocate** **customs** that are not **lawful** for us as Romans to **accept** or practice." The **crowd** **joined** in attacking them, and the magistrates **tore** the garments **off** them and **gave** orders to **beat** them with **rods**. And when they had inflicted **many** **blows** **upon** them, they **threw** them into **prison**, ordering the **jailer** to **keep** them safely. **Having** received this **order**, he put them into the **inner** prison and fastened their **feet** in the **stocks**. (ESV)

```
F B F I J C T I I G P N H C
G T L J R H E S X G K O H K
H S D O R F E C A Z O T O Q
J S W I W I F I J L E N P J
V D R N Z S N G A R I I E O
O R D E R N N C I T Y S S Q
E B D D L I Q E L U F W A L
P V E R V U H P E E K N W U
U T A A S T R A R E T Y J A
L H H G T S M O T S U C E P
P R O G R A F A X P Z Z W A
J E Y E U E C O W N E R S B
D W N D B O U T S T O C K S
Z N A H V P R I S O N F C C
I E M D O S X B K R U I F A
X M A N R M A P C E V F Y B
```

Solution on Page 332

A Feast to the Lord

Exodus 12:14–17

"This **day** **shall** be for you a **memorial** day, and you shall **keep** it as a feast to the **LORD**; throughout your generations, as a **statute** forever, you shall keep it as a feast. **Seven** days you shall **eat** unleavened bread. On the **first** day you shall **remove** leaven **out** of your houses, for if **anyone** eats **what** is leavened, **from** the first day **until** the seventh day, that **person** shall be **cut** **off** from **Israel**. On the first day you shall **hold** a holy **assembly**, and on the seventh day a holy assembly. No **work** shall be **done** on those days. But what everyone **needs** to eat, that **alone** **may** be **prepared** by you. And you shall **observe** the Feast of Unleavened Bread, for on this **very** day I brought your **hosts** out of the **land** of **Egypt**." (ESV)

```
A O M X P C M Z P L J I R H
S D L M K V U G I T X O J I
W G N E V E S T T Z T P S B
F I F F O D N A L P S J X T
E J J Y Z U H O S T S D Q S
Y B S W X S T V Y A M C H O
E Q R B Z W Y T W N P Y Q A
N G D Y W K Q I S R A E L D
M D Y L H E V R E S B O E E
A J Z P A F I R S T N R P K
G S T A T U T E T E A E F S
V K H E V O M E R P R R D H
K E P A D B M J E S O E A T
Y R R R L A I R O M E M H N
F F O Y O L P N E N O D A Y
T L I W H G Q C L P Y G X Y
```

Solution on Page 332

The Importance of Wisdom and Understanding

Proverbs 4:5–12

Get **wisdom**, get understanding; **Forget** not, neither **decline** **from** the **words** of my mouth; **Forsake** her not, and she will **preserve** thee; **Love** her, and she will **keep** thee. Wisdom is the principal thing; therefore get wisdom; **Yea**, with **all** **thy** **getting** get understanding. Exalt her, and she will **promote** thee; She will **bring** thee to **honor**, when thou **dost** **embrace** her. She will **give** to thy **head** a chaplet of **grace**; A **crown** of **beauty** will she **deliver** to thee. Hear, O my **son**, and **receive** my **sayings**; And the years of thy **life** shall be **many**. I have **taught** thee in the **way** of wisdom; I have **led** thee in paths of uprightness. When thou **goest**, thy **steps** shall not be **straitened**; And if thou **runnest**, thou shalt not stumble. (ASV)

46

```
F M A N Y M D O F L A G Q Q
F O L Y S A Y I N G S N S W
I D R U C R O W N H L I O A
R S O G E E V I E C E R N Y
M I N G E S T A P Y D B L B
F W O R D T D R T S O D F J
B J H B E D E C L I N E X Q
B R Z G N S T A U G H T G A
P U L D E L I V E R A O E N
I N E R T M B W Y M E M C V
K N V K I E B S H S O O L Y
H E G G A V V R T C Q R I X
O S E U R S U O A E T P F A
J T T P T A R X L C P A E Y
F Y L M S S C O X L E S D Y
Q K A E G I V E F P A B N Y
```

Solution on Page 333

Jesus Clears the Temple

The Gospel of Matthew 21:12–17

Jesus **went** **into** the **temple** courtyard and **threw** **out** **everyone** who was **buying** and **selling** **there**. He overturned the moneychangers' **tables** and the **chairs** of **those** who sold **pigeons**. He **told** them, "Scripture says, 'My house will be **called** a house of prayer,' but you're **turning** it into a gathering **place** for thieves!" **Blind** and **lame** **people** **came** to him in the temple courtyard, and he healed them. When the **chief** **priests** and the **scribes** **saw** the **amazing** miracles he performed and the children shouting in the temple courtyard, "Hosanna to the **Son** of David!" they were irritated. They said to him, "Do you **hear** **what** these children are saying?" Jesus **replied**, "Yes, I do. Have you **never** **read**, 'From the mouths of **little** children and **infants**, you have created praise'?" He **left** them and went out of the **city** to **Bethany** and **spent** the **night** there. (GW)

```
O T H R E W T W P T S K L F
B H R E A D R A E H H I E G
W E N T J K E S O P T I N D
P R I E S T S L P T H I O L
B E S N V O Z P L C Z E Y O
U U L U F E L E E A S N R T
S R Q B Q A R S M O C D E U
A Y T I C Y N A H T E B V R
Y W C E J O V T V B M G E N
G E H W E N T D S U A P Q I
G N A G T U O I N Y L S O N
D N I G H T S E B I R C S G
B P R L N C A M E N L T P L
M C S I L D T D E G F B E N
Y W H A T E M P L E M O N E
U X L E L F S E L B A T T O
```

Solution on Page 333

A Paralyzed Man Is Forgiven

The Gospel of Mark 2:4–11

Then they **lowered** the **cot** on **which** the **paralyzed man** was **lying**. When **Jesus saw their faith**, he said to the man, "Friend, **your sins** are forgiven." Some **scribes** were **sitting** there. They **thought**, "Why does he **talk** this **way**? He's dishonoring **God**. Who **besides** God **can forgive** sins?" At **once**, Jesus **knew** inwardly **what** they were **thinking**. He **asked** them, "Why do you have these thoughts? Is it **easier** to say to this paralyzed man, 'Your sins are forgiven,' or to say, 'Get up, **pick** up your cot, and walk'? I want you to **know** that the **Son** of Man has **authority** on **earth** to forgive sins." Then he said to the paralyzed man, "I'm **telling** you to get up, pick up your cot, and go home!" (GW)

Solution on Page 333

```
X B F K H W G V K L A T A V
Y Y Q G O T N J G T W H A T
C G T N O E I E A S I E R P
A F K I C M K A C H A I T M
K Y H T R H N R F D O R H L
F F H T C O I X I R N U O R
K M R I R B H F Z P C W U Z
H C H S E A T T O A E O G G
G W A S B D E E U R Y G H N
S W A S K E D Z E A G N T I
T K F U P Y S D P L O I G L
X K L E I B U I N Y S Y V L
M X I Y C O S A D Z N L N E
H A E A K N E W W E I O O T
M X N W K O J Y G D S D O G
M Q O G L F H M A J I C A A
```

Solution on Page 333

Love One Another

Romans 13:8–12

Owe no **man** anything, **save** to **love one** another: for he that loveth his **neighbor** hath fulfilled the **law**. For this, Thou **shalt** not **commit adultery**, Thou shalt not kill, Thou shalt not **steal**, Thou shalt not **covet**, and if there be any other commandment, it is **summed** up in this **word**, **namely**, Thou shalt love **thy** neighbor as thyself. Love worketh no **ill** to his neighbor: love therefore is the fulfilment of the law. And this, **knowing** the season, that **already** it is **time** for you to **awake out** of **sleep**: for now is salvation **nearer** to us than when we **first believed**. The **night** is **far spent**, and the **day** is at **hand**: let us therefore **cast off** the works of darkness, and let us put on the **armor** of **light**. (ASV)

```
L M A N G W E D E F O S D I
A D T W A V Y A N N S Q T X
E V O L A I B D P A E Y D H
T D E S B K N M A M H R W G
S P E N T B E L I E V E D Y
X V E L O H I H V L R T N X
T S A C T B G I S Y D L E Y
Z H T A S W H I R L K U A H
S K H P R F B C N R C D R T
P T G N I W O N K O E A E E
T K I N F M R C V M W O R D
D K L E M I T E M R B E T Y
V Z R I O U T U E A A F D O
H G T L K K S L E E P F J I
S R J L U U I A I Y A O I G
S T D E O H W M M W G I W M P
```

Solution on Page 333

What God Has Done

Ecclesiastes 3:10–14

I have seen the **travail**, **which God hath** given to the **sons** of men to be exercised in it. He hath made every **thing** beautiful in his **time**: also he hath **set** the world in **their** heart, so that no **man can find out** the **work** that God maketh **from** the **beginning** to the **end**. I know that there is no good in them, but for a man to **rejoice**, and to do good in his **life**. And also that every man should **eat** and **drink**, and enjoy the good of **all** his labour, it is the **gift** of God. I know that, whatsoever God **doeth**, it shall be for **ever**: nothing can be put to it, **nor** any thing taken from it: and God doeth it, that men should fear **before** him. (KJV)

Solution on Page 333

```
T W X B Y M C D G I F H T Y
J R E V E U A V K Q A S G L
R N R T L G N I H T E A T G
J H Z G D N I F F R O M U T
A C V A F V S N O S L Z O S
X N S P T L K F N D O L X D
A K H D L R E J O I C E N Z
T Q V A O B A E Z K N I R D
O I E W T G T V P D Z G Y P
H P P Q J H N R A G L P Q P
L R H T E U E W H I C H B G
S I H I O N M K F F L R E E
N O R M S O P E F T R P H Z
U S M E A W L H N V Y X W X
V C T C X N Q N S D O P R T
B Q N M P P M S Z R N P U L
```

Solution on Page 334

Go and Bring Forth Fruit

The Gospel of John 15:16–20

Ye have not **chosen** me, but I have chosen you, and **ordained** you, that ye should go and **bring forth fruit**, and that your fruit should remain: that whatsoever ye **shall ask** of the **Father** in my **name**, he **may give** it you. These **things** I command you, that ye **love one another**. If the world **hate** you, ye know that it hated me before it hated you. If ye were of the world, the world would love his **own**: but **because** ye are not of the world, but I have chosen you **out** of the world, therefore the world hateth you. Remember the **word** that I **said unto** you, The **servant** is not **greater** than his **lord**. If they have persecuted me, they will **also persecute** you; if they have **kept** my **saying**, they will **keep** yours also. (KJV)

```
T P L R C J C T P E K I M G
E N O G V H X J T A K K V Z
E X R I O W O U A D I A S E
Z M D V R U C S H A L L F A
Y P A E R E T A E R G S R A
R T I N S J H I Y N R O U Z
P R N R V U O T L N E P I M
Q Z E A N Y A M O S H E T Y
C P D T V R J C V N T E H L
R T O H T R O F E A A K I X
X U P W J Q E U H B F G N L
H O D Z N C X S A Y I N G Q
Z N Z L S Y I R A F D I S U
L Z W S U E D F D L O R D C
G Z N P N I F H P L T B O P
M U C A V Q W A T N K N Z W
```

Solution on Page 334

The Kingdom of Heaven Is At Hand

The Gospel of Matthew 3:1–7

And in **those** **days** **cometh** **John** the Baptist, preaching in the wilderness of **Judaea**, saying, **Repent** ye; for the **kingdom** of **heaven** is at **hand**. For this is he that was **spoken** of through Isaiah the **prophet**, saying, The **voice** of **one** **crying** in the wilderness, **Make** ye **ready** the **way** of the **Lord**, Make his **paths** straight. Now John **himself** had his **raiment** of camel's **hair**, and a leathern **girdle** about his **loins**; and his **food** was **locusts** and **wild** honey. Then **went** **out** **unto** him Jerusalem, and **all** Judaea, and all the region round about the **Jordan**; and they were baptized of him in the **river** Jordan, confessing **their** **sins**. But when he **saw** **many** of the Pharisees and Sadducees **coming** to his **baptism**, he said unto them, Ye offspring of **vipers**... (ASV)

```
O P C W F L T F N I N E B U
G P I R A L L O C U S T S L
C L C M Y E D E J N C N Y Y
D N O V S I C B U H O E A F
R N M M K I N G D O M W D P
O C I J O O T G A J E O N E
L H N V O E I P E R T Y A K
O B G S H R O N A U H M H V
I X I P D S D I O B B A I U
N N O L H J M A Q R I K R N
S R E T J E R S N R I E H T
P P A K N E V A E H V F H O
O P O T A E S W N I K O R P
K U G D V I P E R S S O T E
E S Y N A M R E C E D D H B
N K X A P S A C R F M R U Z
```

Solution on Page 334

Fools and the Wise

Ecclesiastes 7:5–12

It is **better** to listen to **wise people** who **reprimand** you than to fools who **sing your praises**. The **laughter** of a fool is like the **crackling** of thorns **burning under** a **pot**. Even this is pointless. Oppression **can turn** a wise **person into** a fool, and a **bribe** can **corrupt** the **mind**. The **end** of something is better than its **beginning**. It is better to be patient than **arrogant**. Don't be **quick** to get angry, because **anger** is typical of fools. Don't **ask**, "Why were **things** better in the **old days** than they are now?" It isn't wisdom that **leads** you to ask this! Wisdom is as **good** as an inheritance. It is an **advantage** to **everyone** who **sees** the **sun**. Wisdom **protects** us **just** as **money** protects us, but the advantage of wisdom is that it **gives life** to **those** who have it. (GW)

```
D N G M S E E S E S I A R P
V N L I F E S I W S P E R W
K U E N P R O T E C T S U J
W S A D A T T V K H G O O Z
R E D N U D I E G G N H Y N
T L S I N G V U N O I T O B
O E S G T O A A I O L U E G
S B G Y N L T P N D K R N H
L I P E A I Z N N T C N O Y
R R E L G D H A I C A N Y J
F B F P O N M T G Y R G R L
G E Y O R I I E E P C P E K
V T P E R S O N B X O Z V B
Q T Q P A C O R R U P T E V
C E E G U M K C I U Q S P G
Y R E G N A S K T W B R J Y
```

Solution on Page 334

Win Her Back

Hosea 2:14–18

"That is why I'm **going** to **win** her **back**. I will **lead** her **into** the **desert**. I will **speak tenderly** to her. I will **give** her **vineyards** there. I will **make** the valley of **Achor** a **door** of **hope**. Then she will **respond** as she **did** when she was young, as she did when she came **out** of **Egypt**. On that **day** she will call me her husband," **declares** the LORD. "She will no **longer** call me her **master**. I won't allow her to **say** the **names** of **other gods** called Baal. She will **never again** call out their names. On that day I will make an arrangement with the wild animals, the **birds**, and the animals that **crawl** on the ground. I will **destroy all** the **bows**, **swords**, and **weapons** of **war**, so **people can live** safely." (GW)

Solution on Page 334

```
G R A D D O O R D R G I V E
J N A S D R A Y E N I V G Y
Y E I L I R U H C S E Y O S
L V C O D Y T L L A P R N W
X E T N G O L W A T T O B O
P R A G A I N R R S P I N R
K A A E U D W N E N R E A D
H O T R E S E D S D L W Y S
O U S W O B X F S P N M S L
O T I A T H S N O P A E W Z
C G I D M B C E K S M A T K
Q P L N A C P A T A R Y G F
X J W L K Y V E N C E J O S
X S V C E K R P G W V P D Y
O G A C N Y R O T N I H S F
T B J Y J X R H B G L N B F
```

Solution on Page 335

Ten Lepers

The Gospel of Luke 17:11–19

As **Jesus** continued on **toward** Jerusalem, he **reached** the **border** **between** **Galilee** and Samaria. As he entered a **village** there, **ten lepers stood** at a **distance**, **crying out**, "Jesus, Master, have mercy on us!" He **looked** at them and said, "Go **show** yourselves to the priests." And as they **went**, they were **cleansed** of their **leprosy**. **One** of them, when he **saw** that he was healed, came **back** to Jesus, shouting, "Praise **God**!" He **fell** to the ground at Jesus' **feet**, **thanking** him for **what** he had done. This **man** was a Samaritan. Jesus **asked**, "Didn't I **heal** ten **men**? **Where** are the **other nine**? Has no one **returned** to **give glory** to God **except** this foreigner?" And Jesus said to the man, "Stand up and go. Your **faith** has healed you." (NLT)

```
L Y A C L C V X O M E N E T
A C H G R Z L V O X A V D R
D J S C E Y R E T U R N E D
H U T A H W I G A H S D K P
R D O O T S L N V N R K O E
N O L R O O R I G O S F O Y
M G T G R S L K B K A E L X
V R U Y A L O N C I C P D W
S T O W A R D A T N I N E O
N R M G I S B H A P E D J H
Z F E L L B E T W E E N H S
O L E P R O S Y V K L C W U
Z N R H E I P I S U I T X S
T N E W D L G A K L L E D E
S A H R J T D E H C A E R J
L U W I A L C V D S G F Y F
```

Solution on Page 335

The True Light

The Gospel of John 1:1–9

In the **beginning** was the **Word**, and the Word was with **God**, and the Word was God. The same was in the beginning with God. **All** things were made by him; and **without** him was not any **thing** made that was made. In him was **life**; and the life was the **light** of **men**. And the light **shineth** in **darkness**; and the darkness comprehended it not. There was a **man sent from** God, **whose** name was **John**. The same came for a **witness**, to **bear** witness of the Light, that all men **through** him **might** believe. He was not that Light, but was sent to bear witness of that Light. That was the **true** Light, **which** lighteth **every** man that cometh **into** the world. (KJV)

Solution on Page 335

```
R L O O U O C O M C B E M X
K T T T G D D T R U R E V U
E Y X Z U V A C D T G P L X
D A J F N A M W O R D R T I
W C A Q Q V T E G U A D F Y
K Z N Y C S S T N E S F V F
H M C V D L P A B F S R R X
O G L Q Q S M E O I J O H N
W Z U L D Y V O Z L M P H W
U G Z O A E S P W V I D C W
J B X L R T H I N G G Q I H
I O U Y K H T R X U H L H E
R Z J V N N T U O H T I W S
R S O B E G I N N I N G C A
R Y O S S H I N E T H H B C
X K S W S D H O I V O T N I
```

Solution on Page 335

Jesus Performs Miracles

The Gospel of Matthew 9:27–33

When **Jesus** **left** that **place**, **two** **blind** **men** **followed** him. They shouted, "Have mercy on us, **Son** of David." Jesus **went** **into** a house, and the blind men followed him. He **said** to them, "Do you **believe** that I **can** do this?" "Yes, Lord," they **answered**. He touched **their** **eyes** and said, "What you have believed will be **done** for you!" Then they could **see**. He **warned** them, "Don't let **anyone** **know** about this!" But they went **out** and **spread** the **news** about him throughout that **region**. As they were **leaving**, some **people** brought a **man** to Jesus. The man was **unable** to **talk** because he was possessed by a **demon**. But as soon as the demon was **forced** out, the man **began** to **speak**. The **crowds** were amazed and said, "We have **never** seen **anything** like this in Israel!" (GW)

```
L W Q C P D P M R O S D N R
S U J S I W N Y I W S A J B
A P D C G D E A E T N E K T
C D E H N G M N H Y S R Y F
D R M A Z P F P T U F P E E
Y W O N K V Z H S O E S P L
Z L N W W A I T L V B E Y L
C N O S D N X L E Z O L S X
S F E D G S O I V P B B U K
M A N V D W L D L E C A L P
A K I Y E E L E N O Y N A M
S K K D B R C N A O T U A N
H D F L R E G R J V I N A C
F O I W A D H A O W I G I N
H N P O U T R W F F E N E M
D E I E I V C L Y B K N G R
```

Solution on Page 335

The Wrath of God Against Ungodliness

Romans 1:18–23

For the **wrath** of **God** is revealed **from heaven against all** ungodliness and unrighteousness of **men**, who by **their** unrighteousness suppress the **truth**. For **what can** be **known about** God is **plain** to them, because God has **shown** it to them. For his invisible attributes, namely, his eternal **power** and divine **nature**, have been **clearly** perceived, **ever since** the **creation** of the **world**, in the **things** that have been made. So they are **without excuse**. For although they **knew** God, they **did** not **honor** him as God or **give thanks** to him, but they became **futile** in their thinking, and their foolish **hearts** were **darkened**. **Claiming** to be **wise**, they became **fools**, and exchanged the **glory** of the immortal God for images resembling mortal **man** and **birds** and animals and **creeping** things. (ESV)

```
W N M G L R K N O W N T L T
P E A H N A O P Q X W F W G
M G N I M I A L C I F R O M
E D M K T T P W S H T A R W
N V H A T C L E A R L Y L Z
C X E E T D E N E K R A D L
Y R F R A X V R W R G N W W
C T U U C V D H U A C T N B
B T U U L E E O I T C H O S
H S S O R L F N G K A A G I
S E L I H I S O I T P N N N
G R A O Y T E R A A I K T C
A L L R O U I H E H L S N E
A B O U T F W W T W D P V C
D B I R D S H O W N O I X M
D Y S W Y T W R E K G P D O
```

Solution on Page 336

The Ark and Dagon

1 Samuel 5:1–4

When the Philistines **captured** the **ark** of **God**, they **brought** it **from** **Ebenezer** to **Ashdod**. Then the Philistines **took** the ark of God and brought it **into** the house of Dagon and **set** it up **beside** Dagon. And when the **people** of Ashdod rose early the **next** **day**, **behold**, Dagon had **fallen face** downward on the **ground before** the ark of the **Lord**. So they took Dagon and put him **back** in his **place**. But when they rose early on the next **morning**, behold, Dagon had fallen face downward on the ground before the ark of the Lord, and the **head** of Dagon and **both** his **hands** were **lying cut off** on the **threshold**. **Only** the **trunk** of Dagon was **left** to him. (ESV)

```
B G C P O H F A C E E W E N
C Z T R U N K V A L O F L D
H L U N E X T K P K Z U G O
U E C Y O Z I O T N T E M M
X F A B V U E A U H O H R I
H T S D G N I N R O M T U X
K K H O D L X E E K U O N I
U O D G N T S O D B B B T I
B R O U G H T Z D K E E P U
L E D T O F D Y X H S G K W
D R F L O R A U O Y I Y C T
T A D O O O K L L S D N A H
R W F L R M D N L V E F B D
M F R Q P E O P L E C A L P
A X L Y I N G R O U N D Y N
U P E T N W Q L A O I B D C
```

Solution on Page 336

The Righteous Escape

Proverbs 29:6–14

Evil **people** are trapped by **sin**, but the righteous escape, shouting for **joy**. The **godly** care **about** the **rights** of the **poor**; the **wicked** don't care at **all**. **Mockers** **can** get a whole **town** agitated, but the **wise** will calm **anger**. If a wise **person** **takes** a **fool** to **court**, there will be ranting and ridicule but no satisfaction. The bloodthirsty **hate** blameless people, but the upright **seek** to **help** them. Fools **vent** **their** anger, but the wise **quietly** **hold** it **back**. If a **ruler** **pays** attention to **liars**, all his advisers will be wicked. The poor and the oppressor have this in common—the **LORD** **gives** sight to the **eyes** of **both**. If a **king** **judges** the poor **fairly**, his **throne** will **last** **forever**. (NLT)

Solution on Page 336

```
M L X L E E V Q T A A R M E
V P O O R F U R L Y M W F Y
R E Y R F I E L P O E P G S
X D N D E D E K C I W T P E
Y B O T H V J K Z X R A A E
L P L E H S E G D U J K Y K
D Y O J T R N R O F R E S I
O F A H S A O C O I S S I L
G L G N I K R J E F C R N J
W I S E G U H H A T T K F W
R A V Y L E T I Q U A O F R
M R O E P E R S O N R H W D
K S R V S L L B A C K C V N
D O E I Y O A D S O I R K A
J H O L D O S R L R L N I C
P K N N O F T Z E L G I B G
```

Solution on Page 336

Do Not Cause a Brother to Fall

Romans 14:13–19

Let us not therefore **judge** **one** another any more: but judge ye this rather, that no **man** put a stumblingblock in his brother's **way**, or an occasion of **falling**. I **know**, and am **persuaded** in the **Lord** **Jesus**, that nothing is **unclean** of **itself**: **save** that to him who accounteth anything to be unclean, to him it is unclean. For if **because** of meat **thy** brother is **grieved**, thou walkest no longer in **love**. **Destroy** not with thy meat him for **whom** **Christ** **died**. Let not then **your** good be **evil** **spoken** of: for the **kingdom** of **God** is not **eating** and **drinking**, but righteousness and **peace** and **joy** in the **Holy** **Spirit**. For he that **herein** serveth Christ is well-pleasing to God, and **approved** of **men**. So then let us **follow** **after** things **which** make for peace, and things whereby we may **edify** one another. (ASV)

```
O Y Z S Q K N G M U Y A W X
E E A L R E A T I N G O G M
L V N H K T T D Y C L R X O
E W O O K Z E X V L I G O D
Y J P L W C O U O E R M D G
E S V Y H T R F V A A E N N
G T I R I P S E V N V I I I
D N H H C W D I B O K T E K
U T I Y H E T E R N Y W R N
J G O L S N C P I H L H E O
F F E T L A P R O T C O H W
P E R S U A D E D N S M R P
E O E S R Y F I D E D E I D
Y J E S U S O S K M T S L S
R Y S O O M H J B F Z T H F
W F L W Y G P E A C E V I L
```

Solution on Page 336

I Will Give You Rest

The Gospel of Matthew 11:25–30

At that **time Jesus declared**, "I **thank** you, Father, **Lord** of heaven and **earth**, that you have **hidden these things from** the **wise** and understanding and revealed them to **little children**; **yes**, Father, for **such** was **your gracious** will. **All** things have been **handed over** to me by my Father, and no **one knows** the Son **except** the Father, and no one knows the Father except the Son and anyone to **whom** the Son **chooses** to reveal him. **Come** to me, all who **labor** and are **heavy laden**, and I will **give** you **rest**. **Take** my **yoke** upon you, and learn from me, for I am **gentle** and **lowly** in heart, and you will **find** rest for your **souls**. For my yoke is **easy**, and my **burden** is **light**." (ESV)

Solution on Page 336

```
N N G R C E S L O R D E M E
V J E S U S X S O U L S V E
P L E G Q Y Q B C O M E X E
F I I N D L A D E N B H V K
L V G I O L H Q F H M T L O
E F E H I N B R Q H E A V Y
W O N T S U O I C A R G J U
I G T G R M Y H H N R A V M
S L L D H S I H I D D E N X
E D E R A L C E D E L A S V
Y N E E D H X Y T D Y R U T
K K Z R O C O A L L A T C F
N B E O E U K M W H E H H J
O N S P R E V O D K M A G B
W E T H G I L H Q F I N D Q
S I A I N W Z W O G T K K F
```

Solution on Page 337

The First-Born

Exodus 11:4–8

And **Moses said**, Thus saith **Jehovah**, About midnight will I go **out into** the **midst** of **Egypt**: and **all** the first-born in the **land** of Egypt shall **die**, **from** the first-born of **Pharaoh** that sitteth **upon** his throne, **even unto** the first-born of the maid-servant that is **behind** the **mill**; and all the first-born of **cattle**. And there shall be a **great cry** throughout all the land of Egypt, **such** as there hath not been, **nor** shall be any more. But **against** any of the **children** of **Israel** shall not a **dog move** his **tongue**, against **man** or **beast**: that ye may know how that Jehovah doth make a distinction **between** the Egyptians and Israel. And all these **thy servants** shall **come** down unto me, and **bow** down themselves unto me, **saying**, Get thee out, and all the **people** that **follow** thee: and **after** that I will go out. (ASV)

```
L A Z W T S A E B P J O S O J
R M O S E S T N S H Q Y V S
M B D N A L T N F V N X B P
J I A A P H A R A O H U N J
M E L M M U E G R V L E P U
L F H L A T R S O E R L H L
M X C O F G G L A D M E O G
K R U A V L A R L I V O S W
Y V S Y E A S I T E D E C H
H W Z G W I H D N I H E B R
T L Y M A C N E Z S O L W W
N P E O P L E V N A T T V W
T I X R S W L O W Y N T N E
D U D F T B P M T I I A U U
H A T E Q U N Z I N Y C W O
P P B P L K H E U G N O T D
```

Solution on Page 337

A Foolish Son

Proverbs 17:21–28

The **father** of a **fool** **hath** no **joy**. A **merry** heart **doeth** **good** like a medicine: but a **broken** **spirit** **drieth** the **bones**. A **wicked** **man** **taketh** a **gift** **out** of the bosom to **pervert** the **ways** of **judgment**. Wisdom is **before** him that hath understanding; but the **eyes** of a fool are in the **ends** of the **earth**. A foolish **son** is a **grief** to his father, and bitterness to her that **bare** him. Also to **punish** the **just** is not good, **nor** to **strike** **princes** for **equity**. He that hath knowledge **spareth** his **words**: and a man of understanding is of an excellent spirit. **Even** a fool, when he **holdeth** his **peace**, is counted **wise**: and he that shutteth his **lips** is **esteemed** a man of understanding. (KJV)

Solution on Page 337

```
M E R R Y C K O A R G P J G
R X A D Y D U E T B Q D T F
S P I R I T K G R E Y E S S
B G I F T I I O G F O O L P
J T J I R H K U W O Z H H A
P F A T H E R O Q R T Q S R
Z E S A N S R H T E I R D E
W I C K E D J U D G M E N T
A R G E S N B L U E M G R H
Y G J T X E O A H E C E W E
S D S H N H N T E I V A V V
B U T B A R E T J R N E E C
J A T J N O S S E C N I R P
H G O O D E P P U N I S H W
D Y R E S I W X X A U V R H
O I F O L Z V H H M G U I O
```

Solution on Page 337

I Have Taken Refuge in You

Psalms 71:1–6

I have **taken** **refuge** in you, O **LORD**. Never let me be put to **shame**. Rescue me and **free** me **because** of **your** righteousness. **Turn** your **ear** **toward** me, and **save** me. Be a **rock** on **which** I **may** **live**, a **place** **where** I may **always** go. You **gave** the order to save me! Indeed, you are my rock and my **fortress**. My **God**, free me **from** the **hands** of a **wicked** person, from the **grasp** of **one** who is **cruel** and **unjust**. You are my **hope**, O **Almighty** LORD. You have been my confidence **ever** **since** I was young. I **depended** on you **before** I was **born**. You **took** me from my mother's **womb**. My songs of **praise** constantly speak **about** you. (GW)

```
L J X N B C R U E L I Q C K
F Q U L G M F R O M C K R B
P T D R A W O T O Y C S Y Q
L Y A M X F R W H O P E A R
Q S F K E Q T D R U C V B V
P U K B E D R O J R F E X W
S I N C E N E G U F E R I E
N W R J A S S D P L A C E V
T O O K U L S O N E K R R A
U Z B A I S M B S E F B X G
R L C V L O T I D G P Q J V
N E E O H W A S G W H E R E
B M U C I R A B L H A N D S
U A I L P V Q Y O N T O R E
V H F N E Q I R S U C Y O S
W S O P W P R P P P V T D L L
```

Solution on Page 337

Warning to the Rich

James 5:1–6

Come now, you **rich**, **weep** and **howl** for the miseries that are coming **upon** you. Your riches have **rotted** and your **garments** are moth-eaten. Your **gold** and **silver** have **corroded**, and **their corrosion** will be **evidence against** you and will **eat** your **flesh** like fire. You have **laid** up treasure in the **last** days. Behold, the **wages** of the **laborers** who **mowed** your **fields**, **which** you **kept back** by **fraud**, are **crying out** against you, and the **cries** of the **harvesters** have reached the ears of the **Lord** of hosts. You have **lived** on the earth in **luxury** and in self-indulgence. You have **fattened** your hearts in a **day** of slaughter. You have **condemned** and murdered the righteous **person**. He does not **resist** you. (ESV)

Solution on Page 337

Puzzles

```
U R D P J L W O H C I H W K
P G L D P O L E B L R U C F
O M O W E D E N E T T A F S
N T G C C V T V F P B D T L
G D W R M S I S C I E N U D
P C I Y N D R L X T E X Y P
Z E O I E N Q E T M U L A E
S N A N O I S O R R O C D R
L G C G D E R A Y O U T D S
A E E N G E G T C H B E S O
I N X A F F M O S C L A I N
D J W R T A M N M I A F L K
H H A R V E S T E R S L V E
N U C O R R O D E D T E E P
D R O L Q Z U H X W H S R T
A J I G U N A R R I E H T I
```

Solution on Page 338

Ruth Marries Boaz

Ruth 4:13–17

So **Boaz took Ruth**, and she **became** his **wife**. And he **went** in to her, and the **LORD gave** her **conception**, and she **bore** a **son**. Then the **women said** to **Naomi**, "Blessed be the LORD, who has not **left** you this **day without** a **redeemer**, and **may** his **name** be **renowned** in **Israel**! He **shall** be to you a **restorer** of **life** and a **nourisher** of **your old age**, for your daughter-in-law who **loves** you, who is more to you than **seven** sons, has **given birth** to him." Then Naomi took the **child** and laid him on her **lap** and became his **nurse**. And the women of the neighborhood gave him a name, **saying**, "A son has been born to Naomi." They named him **Obed**. He was the **father** of **Jesse**, the father of David. (ESV)

```
D L O U E P L A P X J L C H
B O A Z Q O R H M Y R N B R
X V I S R A E L T F E L G G
E E D D R E H S I R U O N T
E S S E J N T A N E I F O D
S A Y I N G A B U D C B I H
D H T N E W F M G E R A T F
A U A N E M O W E E S U P B
E F I L A W K N R M R G E V
W A P Y L O C O E E N C C Q
U N T U O H T I W R A E N G
S N B T I S K N Y M O N O S
Q B U L E N E V E S M B C U
A B D R U O Y G V V I Z W E
E A S K S O H I A W I F E I
Y T E C D E B O G F X G A H
```

Solution on Page 338

Cherish Wisdom

Proverbs 4:2–9

After **all**, I have **taught** you **well**. Do not **abandon** my teachings. When I was a **boy** **learning** **from** my **father**, when I was a **tender** and **only** **child** of my **mother**, they **used** to **teach** me and **say** to me, "Cling to my **words** wholeheartedly. **Obey** my commands so that you **may** **live**. **Acquire** **wisdom**. Acquire understanding. Do not **forget**. Do not **turn** **away** from the words that I have **spoken**. Do not abandon wisdom, and it will **watch** over you. **Love** wisdom, and it will **protect** you. The **beginning** of wisdom is to acquire wisdom. Acquire understanding with all that you have. **Cherish** wisdom. It will **raise** you up. It will **bring** you **honor** when you **embrace** it. It will **give** you a **graceful** **garland** for **your** head." (GW)

```
B O Y J E Z F M W H G S H W
V Y B C N R E H T O M E H M
T B S E O G S M O Y L N O G
S U D M Y A W A B A N D O N
R L R Z H C U D Y R S R G I
Y R O N O H G E S I A R I N
O K W V V E P N W Z F C V N
U I K Q E R R Y I O S T E I
R W E G T I O I R N H S J G
N E K O P S T G U G R Y R E
G L D V Q H E V U Q H A Q B
N L C N B T C A Y A C L E A
X T H R E H T A F E A A O L
V L I V E T M T F D E S U L
X N L G N R E U W A T C H Q
G C D G A R L A N D L U L R
```

Solution on Page 338

King of Kings

Revelation 19:16–20

On his clothes and his **thigh** he has a **name** **written**: **King** of Kings and **Lord** of Lords. I **saw** an **angel** standing in the **sun**. He **cried** **out** in a loud **voice** to **all** the **birds** **flying** overhead, "Come! Gather for the great **banquet** of **God**. **Eat** the **flesh** of kings, generals, warriors, horses and **their** riders, and all **free** **people** and **slaves**, **both** important or insignificant people." I saw the beast, the kings of the earth, and their armies gathered to wage **war** **against** the **rider** on the **horse** and his **army**. The beast and the false **prophet** who had **done** miracles for the beast were **captured**. By these miracles the false prophet had **deceived** **those** who had the **brand** of the beast and worshiped its **statue**. Both of them were **thrown** alive **into** the **fiery** **lake** of **burning** sulfur. (GW)

```
D O U C W U J J U H T P F K V
E C I O V B H X T H V H L E
C A P T U R E D O E G S U P
E W G N I Y L F B I D T R N
I R L A K E T U H R A O N K
V I W O I W R T I T P L B Q
E T E U Q N A B S H S E L F
D T M T I F S R E D O N E A
T E A N G E L T V L O R D K
V N G I W Y M R A Y P E S V
X Q U V D O G B L V R O D E
K M M Q C X R L S E E E E K
Y H P E M A N H D S D E I P
H W A S N H X I T O U N R F
Z T J D I Q R D V H G N C F
T V E N G R G Q O T N I C C
```

Solution on Page 338

Take a Lesson from the Ants

Proverbs 6:6–15

Take a **lesson** **from** the **ants**, you lazybones. **Learn** from **their** **ways** and **become** **wise**! Though they have no **prince** or governor or **ruler** to **make** them **work**, they **labor** **hard** **all** **summer**, gathering **food** for the winter. But you, lazybones, how **long** will you **sleep**? When will you **wake** up? A **little** **extra** sleep, a little more slumber, a little folding of the **hands** to rest—then poverty will **pounce** on you like a **bandit**; scarcity will **attack** you like an **armed** **robber**. **What** are worthless and wicked **people** like? They are constant **liars**, signaling their **deceit** with a **wink** of the **eye**, a **nudge** of the foot, or the wiggle of fingers. Their perverted **hearts** **plot** **evil**, and they constantly **stir** up trouble. But they will be destroyed suddenly. (NLT)

```
L S T R A E H S Y A W D R V
H E H R L T T A K E E I C V
A Y M T O I T B B C Y I S F
R E T L R D E A E P Q B T E
D I P X K N X I C T E N U L
L F W W J A T K O K C V T M
B L H Q L B R P M L N D I W
E W U Q E U A F E W I J R L
G G N O L Y E S C O R C O V
A F S E S G S S N L P R B Q
D R R T D O N L U V I L B Y
V O I U N R T E O M X A E K
T M N E A A K E P D M O R K
A L K E H A N P Q L O E R S
Y A L W W T I D L A B O R P
M K D C Y K W A S T W H F R
```

Solution on Page 339

Love Your Enemies

The Gospel of Matthew 5:43–48

"You have **heard** that it was said, 'You **shall** **love** **your** **neighbor** and **hate** your enemy.' But I **say** to you, Love your **enemies** and **pray** for **those** who **persecute** you, so that you **may** be **sons** of your **Father** who is in heaven. For he makes his **sun** **rise** on the **evil** and on the **good**, and **sends** **rain** on the **just** and on the unjust. For if you love those who love you, what **reward** do you have? Do not **even** the **tax** **collectors** do the same? And if you **greet** **only** your brothers, what more are you **doing** than **others**? Do not even the **Gentiles** do the same? You **therefore** **must** be **perfect**, as your heavenly Father is perfect." (ESV)

```
E A O G A L B F Y X X N W T
C S O N L Y T A E A B U C R
D O I N G A O T H E R S Q L
D F L R C M U H T Z V P X H
E Y W L I C C E I G C H N F
D R A W E R B R E V I L V F
S O N S S C H N J U S T L G
N X R K X T T A R S H T B G
T E T F K I T O T E E R G A
P C V C L F B S R E S N Q U
J I B E E H N E G S O P D T
Q S S D G F F I V Z H Y A S
L I P I M O R M A O T B H U
M M E V R U I E L R L A O M
R N X E O E H N P S L Q X O
S U I Y D R A E H L G R G Y
```

Solution on Page 339

Love the Lord Your God

Deuteronomy 6:3–8

"**Hear** therefore, O **Israel**, and be **careful** to do them, that it **may** go **well** with you, and that you may **multiply** **greatly**, as the **LORD**, the **God** of **your** fathers, has **promised** you, in a **land** **flowing** with **milk** and honey. Hear, O Israel: The LORD our God, the LORD is **one**. You shall **love** the LORD your God with **all** your heart and with all your **soul** and with all your **might**. And **these** **words** that I command you **today** shall be on your heart. You shall **teach** them diligently to your **children**, and shall talk of them when you **sit** in your **house**, and when you walk by the **way**, and when you **lie** **down**, and when you **rise**. You shall **bind** them as a sign on your **hand**, and they shall be as frontlets **between** your **eyes**." (ESV)

```
I G Z R I X K D Z Z V U D H
X U W B T H G I M O N E D B
S K H I D O R L F G S T Y G
R Q S W C N E M L U E O O M
Q U B R A G A S O E C D L X
B N S U H Y T H W H W A W Z
T K L I M U L T I P L Y S S
X W S F L O Y L N B U K E N
N K P O R P D Y G R F Y Y J
V M V D P R O M I S E D D T
B E T W E E N S S E R N E T
I N F N S D E Q R R A A N E
N T A W O R D S A L C L I D
D L K W U D X E E H A L F B
J A N O L Y H R L H G L W O
Z R Y M K X H D Y V T N I B
```

Solution on Page 339

Children Through Faith

Galatians 3:24–29

Let me put it another **way**. The **law** was our **guardian** **until** **Christ** **came**; it **protected** us until we **could** be **made** **right** with **God** **through** **faith**. And now that the way of faith has **come**, we no longer need the law as our guardian. For you are **all** **children** of God through faith in Christ Jesus. And all who have been **united** with Christ in **baptism** have put on Christ, like **putting** on **new** clothes. **There** is no longer **Jew** or **Gentile**, slave or **free**, male and female. For you are all one in Christ Jesus. And now that you **belong** to Christ, you are the **true** children of **Abraham**. You are his **heirs**, and God's **promise** to Abraham belongs to you. (NLT)

Solution on Page 339

```
E C G S X C H P G Q T Q N M
A S O Y L H S V M E M D N M
P P I U Z I T U X H Q W Y O
W U R M L L Z I I J N U T Y
A P T O O D Q C A M E N H B
F M Y T T R N B I F P T E W
E R P E I E P A O G K I R A
G L E B W N C P G N O L E B
S Z C E E E G T L A W D X Y
A N J T L D Q I E I I A L L
Y U E C S I A S S D B T L Q
O N Y Y T I T M Y R U R E Z
K I A O S H R N A A I U D J
W T H R O U G H E U W E J R
C E E K R V A I C G N F H Q
D D G C O M E I R G J K O T
```

Solution on Page 339

The Church Grows

Acts 2:41–47

They then that **received** his **word** were **baptized**: and there were **added** **unto** them in that **day** **about** **three** thousand souls. And they continued stedfastly in the **apostles'** **teaching** and **fellowship**, in the breaking of **bread** and the **prayers**. And **fear** **came** upon **every** **soul**: and many wonders and **signs** were done through the apostles. And **all** that believed were together, and had all **things** common; and they **sold** **their** possessions and goods, and **parted** them to all, according as any **man** had **need**. And day by day, continuing stedfastly with **one** **accord** in the **temple**, and breaking bread at **home**, they **took** their **food** with **gladness** and singleness of **heart**, praising **God**, and **having** **favor** with all the **people**. And the **Lord** added to them day by day **those** that were **saved**. (ASV)

```
C D P A O T N U U D F M Z D
T R S D E G H L E E E O A O
L I B D R N H O M E A Y O N
D E B E E I O V S N R G Q D
D H W D M V F S C E N H I D
E T U O B A I X V I V P T P
W S Y G V H C E H Y S I P R
A O E O E X E C C G N H E A
B L R A G L A D N E S S O Y
P D R D P E R I F T R W P E
A T A M T O H P Q D R O L R
G A E E C T A P O S T L E S
G T F C R R O Z S O U L Q N
T O A S T B A P T I Z E D G
B O D E V A S L W A L F G I
F K D W P H Q H L V G A X S
```

Solution on Page 340

The Power of Sin Is Broken

Romans 6:3–7

Don't you **know** that **all** of us who were **baptized into Christ Jesus** were baptized into his **death**? When we were baptized into his death, we were **placed** into the **tomb** with him. As Christ was **brought back from** death to **life** by the **glorious power** of the **Father**, so we, too, **should live** a **new kind** of life. If we've become **united** with him in a death like his, **certainly** we will also be united with him when we **come** back to life as he did. We know that the **person** we **used** to be was **crucified** with him to put an **end** to **sin** in our bodies. Because of this we are no **longer slaves** to sin. The person who has **died** has been **freed** from sin. (GW)

```
F O E K Q Z E N V Y T Y P N
H S Y T Q O I F S F S X L A
D B L O Y S L A V E S O A A
Z I N M D D O T Q S N D C K
I S I B E E E H S G N L E A
Q Z A A G W E E E I S U D X
S C T C E B O R U I R O T J
F H R K Z A L N F B F H E K
J E E U G P I G K T G S C C
K I C S C T M L C U U R X U
S L I V E I M O O S S Y B Z
D I E D Y Z F R R W E N G W
N N C S Z E B I E F D V X Q
I T Y O F D N O E W H N L B
K O I I M Y Z U A D O J E G
A L L C P E R S O N A P F G
```

Solution on Page 340

A Throne Set in Heaven

Revelation 4:2–6

Straightway I was in the **Spirit**: and **behold**, there was a throne set in heaven, and **one sitting** upon the throne; and he that **sat** was to **look** upon like a **jasper** stone and a sardius: and there was a **rainbow** round about the throne, like an **emerald** to look upon. And round about the throne were four and **twenty** thrones: and upon the thrones I saw four and twenty **elders** sitting, **arrayed** in white **garments**; and on **their heads crowns** of gold. And **out** of the throne **proceed lightnings** and **voices** and **thunders**. And there were seven **lamps** of **fire burning before** the throne, **which** are the seven Spirits of **God**; and before the throne, as it were a **sea** of **glass** like a **crystal**; and in the **midst** of the throne, and round about the throne, four **living creatures full** of **eyes** before and **behind**. (ASV)

```
U I F B E H O L D V B D R P
A S U V K V D N L U L O O K
M Y L I O S I A R Q M G U H
M T L I G H T N I N G S I Q
I N C O E S I N E L D E R S
D E G B Y N F N E C T R V P
S W M R G S O D A M O U T I
T T C E P W E W E C R T J R
W C G K R R O W C Y H A Z I
H F K C O A T B G U A E G T
I U I F C H L O N L T R H H
C R E R E S D D I I A C R E
H B Y I E A E S T L A M O A
T J R Y D R R V T A S R P D
I R E P S A J L I V I N G S
Q H D C R O W N S S A L G W
```

Solution on Page 340

Jesus Sends the Twelve

The Gospel of Mark 6:6–13

Then **Jesus** **went** **from** village to village, teaching the **people**. And he **called** his twelve disciples together and **began** sending them **out** **two** by two, **giving** them authority to **cast** out **evil** spirits. He **told** them to **take** nothing for **their** journey **except** a walking stick—no **food**, no traveler's **bag**, no **money**. He allowed them to **wear** sandals but not to take a **change** of clothes. "Wherever you go," he **said**, "stay in the same house **until** you **leave** **town**. But if any **place** refuses to welcome you or **listen** to you, **shake** its **dust** from your **feet** as you leave to **show** that you have abandoned **those** people to their fate." So the disciples went out, telling everyone they **met** to repent of their **sins** and **turn** to **God**. And they cast out **many** demons and **healed** many **sick** people, anointing them with **olive** **oil**. (NLT)

```
O I Q X R M W U E R E O E M
S E M I I Z U L X I C N J E
D T U O C N R V L E A V E T
U I E G N A H C I H L L S N
I N C I U E L J S T P U U R
Q T T V F N Y L T O D D S U
O E V I L O M A E X C E P T
B E S N L I K P N D C L K N
D F Y G V E O F B E G A N E
L B V V A O M V O K B E S W
R V N S W B F Y N A M H W T
R P G W D X Z S E H W E D K
X K X T O L D I A S A O U C
S T O W G T P N F R O M H I
T O T G F D R S Q F W H L S
S S L O O T B A K Y P W T Q
```

Solution on Page 340

Even the Sea Obeys Him

The Gospel of Mark 4:36–41

Leaving the **crowd**, they **took Jesus along** in a **boat just** as he was. **Other** boats were with him. A **violent** windstorm **came** up. The **waves** were **breaking into** the boat so that it was **quickly filling** up. But he was **sleeping** on a **cushion** in the **back** of the boat. So they **woke** him up and **said** to him, "Teacher, don't you **care** that we're **going** to die?" Then he got up, **ordered** the **wind** to **stop**, and said to the **sea**, "Be **still**, **absolutely** still!" The wind stopped blowing, and the sea became **very calm**. He **asked** them, "Why are you **such cowards**? Don't you have any **faith** yet?" They were overcome with **fear** and asked **each** other, "Who is this **man**? **Even** the wind and the sea **obey** him!" (GW)

```
U K S P O T S F K E O W T E
S O D W L U U A O C X O U U
O E I A Q W S B F R Z K I G
L N A D C K E V I O L E N T
D H S P E Y J E O W L I T D
Q C Y D B R N R T D V S O J
D U E L R F E Y H A U A K Y
N S I C E A I D E J K S C F
O U G C A T W L R N O T A T
E W D N K M U O L O O I B W
N C A G I L E L C I T L E C
J M B G N P Y D O H N L G X
G N I O G O E F D S N G Z H
F E A R A R L E Y U B Y C C
R V U O A T R A L C C A L M
U E D C W W A V E S E V N M
```

Solution on Page 341

Trip to Bethlehem

The Gospel of Luke 2:1–7

Now it **came** to **pass** in **those days**, **there** **went** **out** a **decree** **from** **Caesar** **Augustus**, that **all** the **world** should be enrolled. This was the **first** enrolment **made** when Quirinius was **governor** of **Syria**. And all went to **enrol** themselves, **every** **one** to his **own city**. And **Joseph** also went up from Galilee, out of the city of **Nazareth**, into **Judaea**, to the city of **David**, **which** is called **Bethlehem**, **because** he was of the house and **family** of David; to enrol **himself** with **Mary**, who was betrothed to him, being **great** with **child**. And it came to pass, while they were there, the days were fulfilled that she should be delivered. And she brought **forth** her firstborn son; and she **wrapped** him in swaddling clothes, and **laid** him in a **manger**, because there was no **room** for them in the **inn**. (ASV)

```
D C G L Q K Q N Y Q T O W N
O I A F O R T H F R Q I H H
O I P M C E B Y P I A L I A
D V T O E M A N G E R M C V
S T N R L S Y A D U S S H U
Q T U F O L O R N E S O T R
F H U M W O A H L S A U J N
W E V E R Y M F T U P T R A
O R T F A M I L Y A F A A Z
R E D M P U S J S C S N H A
L G L E P E G O V E R N O R
D C I T E S G U A B E P M E
A L H R D W R C S Y R I A T
V E C M E H E L H T E B D H
I E N N I P A E A D U J E I
D I T O A Y T I C R H S Q B
```

Solution on Page 341

Spreading the Good News

The Gospel of Luke 4:40–44

As the **sun went down** that evening, **people** throughout the **village** brought **sick family members** to Jesus. No **matter what** their **diseases** were, the touch of his **hand healed every** one. Many were possessed by **demons**; and the demons **came out** at his **command**, shouting, "You are the **Son** of **God**!" But **because** they **knew** he was the **Messiah**, he **rebuked** them and **refused** to let them **speak**. Early the **next morning** Jesus went out to an isolated **place**. The **crowds** searched everywhere for him, and when they **finally** found him, they **begged** him not to **leave** them. But he replied, "I **must preach** the Good News of the **Kingdom** of God in **other towns**, too, because that is why I was sent." So he continued to **travel** around, preaching in synagogues throughout **Judea**. (NLT)

```
S O K V A U Q H C A E R P N
S N W O T H E R E T T A M Z
I W L X E U B T N A E S Q G
G O E M P E O P L E L H U P
C D A H G F N S N O M E D M
F C V G N I N R O M W A D S
Y R E V E E D E K U B E R I
E D B X C F T B H S C D N C
S P E A K R B M G O O U H K
V I L L A G E E M G K J A P
D P B V D Y C M O D G N I K
I L E Y L L A N I F E X S D
N L K I N N U C R O W D S Y
P U M O D E S U F E R N E W
Q A S E S A E S I D Z A M N
F W E N T X E N A R W H A T
```

Solution on Page 341

A Temple of God

1 Corinthians 3:16–23

Do you not **know** that you are **God**'s **temple** and that God's **Spirit dwells** in you? If anyone destroys God's temple, God will **destroy** him. For God's temple is **holy**, and you are that temple. Let no **one deceive himself**. If anyone among you thinks that he is **wise** in this **age**, let him become a **fool** that he **may** become wise. For the wisdom of this **world** is **folly** with God. For it is **written**, "He **catches** the wise in **their** craftiness," and again, "The **Lord** knows the **thoughts** of the wise, that they are futile." So let no one **boast** in **men**. For **all things** are **yours**, whether **Paul** or **Apollos** or **Cephas** or the world or **life** or **death** or the **present** or the future—all are yours, and you are **Christ**'s, and Christ is God's. (ESV)

```
P N B P J Q X Y C Z H W H F
H X R F Q Q F U W F H O H B
L A H Z A U Z T H E I R L G
H U S D W O H O W L P L O Y
F B A T N E S E R P O D E Y
W C E P H A S F C M A O L K
D H N S R O L I A E P L F U
Y R O O D M U L T T O J Q G
M I O E U D V G C F L H W F
F S A L W E D Z H N L P L K
V T D E C E I V E T O E Y S
H M L E S I W T S Z S O G M
B L U T S L T N E M U N E A
S Z R N D I S P I R I T L Y
L O H A R J Y H S H N L K V
Y W R W O N K Q T S A O B E
```

Solution on Page 341

Paul Shook the Dust

Acts 18:4–8

Each Sabbath **found Paul** at the synagogue, **trying** to convince the **Jews** and **Greeks** alike. And **after Silas** and Timothy **came** down **from** Macedonia, Paul **spent all** his **time** preaching the **word**. He testified to the Jews that **Jesus** was the **Messiah**. But when they opposed and insulted him, Paul **shook** the **dust** from his clothes and **said**, "**Your blood** is **upon** your **own** heads—I am innocent. From now on I will go preach to the Gentiles." Then he **left** and **went** to the **home** of **Titius Justus**, a **Gentile** who worshiped **God** and **lived next door** to the synagogue. **Crispus**, the **leader** of the synagogue, and everyone in his household believed in the **Lord**. **Many others** in **Corinth** also **heard** Paul, became believers, and were baptized. (NLT)

```
I N K R L Q D A K Z W B N P
I E C E E D U S U T S U J A
J X F T M D Y K U T K E M F
A T L F K S A E N P W E O F
D V H A U T N E W S S L C A
D I A S H Y P R L S H I O P
X I E G R S N G I D O T R W
S J K D G E M A C E O N I C
M N O N N W H S M V K E N D
O O S U I T I T I I L G T O
R P B O Y T D O O L B P H H
F U K F R O W N A E A E Y V
H E M I T S U D L U A S I Q
A H D S R H R R L R C C G R
G R U Z U O S O D E M O H H
X X H Y W M Y L C I D W W Z
```

Solution on Page 342

Water from the Rock

Exodus 17:2–6

So they complained to Moses by **saying**, "Give us **water** to drink!" Moses **said** to them, "Why are you complaining to me? Why are you **testing** the **Lord**?" But the **people** were **thirsty** for water **there**. They complained to Moses and **asked**, "Why **did** you **bring** us **out** of **Egypt**? Was it to **make** us, our **children**, and our livestock die of thirst?" So Moses **cried** out to the Lord, "What should I do with these people? They're almost **ready** to **stone** me!" The Lord **answered** Moses, "Bring **some** of the **leaders** of **Israel** with you, and go to **where** the people **can** **see** you. **Take** the **staff** you used to **strike** the **Nile** **River**. I'll be standing in **front** of you there by a **rock** at Mount **Horeb**. Strike the rock, and water will **come** out of it for the people to drink." (GW)

Solution on Page 342

```
U R C L J M S I R T D L X X
E P B D A H J T H E N O T S
G R B K X M P I R S A R X D
S P E W I G R E R T D D R R
F I U H K S W E Q I E I Y Q
D A N P T S D L D N D A S F
C D T Y N A N P C G E S C U
I F P A E K I O P O W G T P
Z G Y L R X L E R A N A O M
C G G T D H E P T I S L I F
T F E N L K D E Y K V O B S
G F N O I S R A E L Y E M E
L A L R H R S D E I R C R E
C T T F C U B M S O M E O K
W S P S T U O X H V H X C A
C D B E N C X Q N W N D K T
```

Solution on Page 342

Abide in Me

The Gospel of John 15:3–7

Already you are **clean** because of the **word** that I have **spoken** to you. **Abide** in me, and I in you. As the **branch** cannot **bear fruit** by **itself**, **unless** it abides in the **vine**, **neither can** you, unless you abide in me. I am the vine; you are the branches. **Whoever** abides in me and I in him, he it is that bears **much** fruit, for **apart from** me you can do **nothing**. If **anyone** does not abide in me he is **thrown away** like a branch and **withers**; and the branches are **gathered**, thrown **into** the **fire**, and **burned**. If you abide in me, and my words abide in you, **ask whatever** you **wish**, and it will be **done** for you. (ESV)

Solution on Page 342

```
S R E H T I W A F C P E E R
N D C A X N H P G H N Y D Y
W U I A L S A A S F L E R J
M Z T Y I R T R E F N A O D
S A C W L H E T H R V A W N
Q I S T E O V A U O F N U K
M F S R X C E B D M Z Y D Z
F L E S T I R V R Y R O R N
R D L J P A N E Z C A N A R
U H N L N O V T H K O E E E
I C U C O E K O O T L L B N
T T H R O W N E H C I T V S
V A O H W K D I N S L E I O
M M W S S I N O E O Z W N F
K V F A B G D J N L K E E T
A Y P A Y Q X V Z E R I F J
```

Solution on Page 342

Costly Ointment

The Gospel of Mark 14:3–8

And **while** he was in **Bethany** in the **house** of **Simon** the **leper**, as he **sat** at **meat**, **there** came a **woman** **having** an alabaster **cruse** of ointment of **pure nard** very **costly**; and she **brake** the cruse, and **poured** it **over** his **head**. But there were **some** that had indignation **among** themselves, saying, To what purpose **hath** this **waste** of the ointment been **made**? For this ointment **might** have been **sold** for above **three hundred** shillings, and **given** to the **poor**. And they murmured **against** her. But **Jesus** said, Let her **alone**; why **trouble** ye her? She hath **wrought** a **good work** on me. For ye have the poor **always** with you, and whensoever ye will ye **can** do them good: but me ye have not always. She hath **done** what she **could**. (ASV)

```
O M N O E L B U O R T N B Y
Q E H X D E R D N U H A V S
U A T S T H G I M T O F O D
A T W H E R B C W G L L N L
N S A O G N I V A H D A H U
J N D E R U O P S I M O N O
Y I Z S W K O D Y L T S O C
C A N U M W G R A L O N E G
F G U R A S O M W E B S R P
M A J C D J O M L R U Q E T
I G I V E N A I A O B D H I
B T V S G L H K H N R R T J
B K U A K W E E D A E H H T
N S P M Z A M P N E T S A W
H B R M P O O R E V O S T X
J I S L S D T P U R E E H D
```

Solution on Page 342

An Angel Appears

The Gospel of Luke 1:26–33

In the **sixth** **month** of Elizabeth's pregnancy, **God** sent the **angel** **Gabriel** to Nazareth, a **village** in **Galilee**, to a **virgin** named Mary. She was engaged to be married to a **man** named **Joseph**, a descendant of **King** **David**. Gabriel **appeared** to her and **said**, "Greetings, favored woman! The **Lord** is with you!" Confused and disturbed, Mary **tried** to **think** **what** the angel **could** **mean**. "Don't be **afraid**, Mary," the angel **told** her, "for you have **found** **favor** with God! You will **conceive** and **give** **birth** to a **son**, and you will **name** him **Jesus**. He will be very **great** and will be **called** the Son of the **Most** **High**. The Lord God will give him the **throne** of his **ancestor** David. And he will **reign** **over** **Israel** forever; his Kingdom will never **end**!" (NLT)

```
Q P K A D G O D I F S B P M
Y F G F N B I A S A C O W H
W T F R U I K V R M J D C W
G Q H A O R N I A L E I H O
C V F I F T A D E L L A C V
I Z I D N H S D L E T S N E
L J G R H K D E I R T Q V R
B N O R G R V R C A K I N G
V N O S E I B A O N G D N E
L H I I E A N E U G A L B W
O T G C G P T P L E L O D S
R N N H G I H P D L I T U I
D O A V I L L A G E L S Z X
C M V M X T H R O N E O A T
E Y A A E A Z M W J E M I H
P D E U F G F F J V W B W O
```

Solution on Page 343

The New Heaven and Earth

Revelation 21:1–4

And I **saw** a **new** **heaven** and a new earth: for the **first** heaven and the first earth are passed **away**; and the **sea** is no more. And I saw the **holy** **city**, new Jerusalem, **coming** **down** **out** of heaven of **God**, **made** ready as a **bride** adorned for her **husband**. And I heard a **great** **voice** out of the throne saying, Behold, the **tabernacle** of God is with **men**, and he **shall** **dwell** with them, and they shall be his **peoples**, and God himself shall be with them, and be **their** God: and he shall **wipe** away **every** **tear** **from** their **eyes**; and **death** shall be no more; neither shall there be mourning, **nor** **crying**, nor **pain**, any more: the first **things** are passed away. (ASV)

Solution on Page 343

```
C N R E P I W S X T J H J S
N L E M D P O D O W N E W E
E L L V G I S G N I Y R C P
D E L C A N R E B A T T S B
A W A Y G E I B L V B W I Y
M D H X T N H M A P T S R C
J M S K T A W T O C O E U T
S E A R D H E S A C V E E H
O X W A Y I E R N E A C P I
N A J F N I A I G A D I I N
J N F I A E A F R Y G O D G
R L U E T P J B R L M V O S
C M I G N T S M O O U T U E
A V T L S X F C N H M E N Y
I Q U H S K A H A S K D F E
H J W Z L Z I A B M I D W Y
```

Solution on Page 343

The Star

The Gospel of Matthew 2:7–12

Then **Herod** summoned the **wise men** secretly and ascertained **from** them **what** time the **star** had appeared. And he **sent** them to Bethlehem, saying, "Go and **search** diligently for the **child**, and when you have **found** him, **bring** me **word**, that I too **may** come and worship him." **After** listening to the **king**, they **went** on **their way**. And **behold**, the star that they had **seen** when it **rose** went **before** them **until** it came to **rest over** the **place** where the child was. When they **saw** the star, they rejoiced exceedingly with **great joy**. And **going into** the **house** they saw the child with Mary his mother, and they **fell** down and worshiped him. Then, opening their treasures, they offered him **gifts**, **gold** and frankincense and **myrrh**. And **being** warned in a **dream** not to **return** to Herod, they departed to their **own** country by another way. (ESV)

```
P I Q F E R T E T E F N N N L T
K T P O U D L D R B R Q E L
E U F M R F M P L A C E M R
N M H O N Y A W T H R R Y M
G W W O U J E S I Z M G O W
R O E H U N R L K B D O J B
O E L N O S D L O H E B R F
M Z V D T R E T U R N I J F
D T M O N R N F O E N U N K
I S A R I E T F M G L P I G
D E Y E S S E A R C H L O D
J R H H R B S E E N H I E K
I T O O B G I F T S N T I F
S X S T W L F B F G A N L R
X E H K A N T X A H G U V Z
J Z J V S U P M W I S E O R
```

Solution on Page 343

Hailstorm

Exodus 9:22–25

Then the **LORD** **said** to **Moses**, "Stretch **out** your **hand** **toward** heaven, so that **there** may be **hail** in **all** the **land** of **Egypt**, on **man** and **beast** and every plant of the **field**, in the land of Egypt." Then Moses stretched out his **staff** toward heaven, and the LORD **sent** **thunder** and hail, and **fire** **ran** **down** to the **earth**. And the LORD rained hail **upon** the land of Egypt. There was hail and fire **flashing** continually in the **midst** of the hail, **very** **heavy** hail, **such** as had never been in all the land of Egypt **since** it **became** a **nation**. The hail **struck** down everything that was in the field in all the land of Egypt, **both** man and beast. And the hail struck down every plant of the field and **broke** every **tree** of the field. (ESV)

```
J X D J J S G G E S U C H P
Q Y G G Y P B Y V E R Y B R
V E E X D L T Y S N R E Y R
Z K Z N G K C U R T S T Z J
U Q J P O J N T O H A L L A
F C S C B N N Y W U A F J B
J N S F L A S H I N G N F O
G U E F T R D M I D S T D H
U P S I K N I T T E A R T H
H O O E A T U S M R C P Z H
G N M L T O W A R D F N F Q
L S I D H L C E G Y P T I T
M A N F O E C B R O K E R S
H I Z R B W A H I E D E E U
Z D D O K X N V A Y H T O B
Z E Q H A N F A Y C R T F O
```

Solution on Page 343

Remain Steadfast

James 1:12–17

Blessed is the **man** who remains steadfast **under trial**, for when he has **stood** the **test** he will receive the crown of **life**, **which God** has promised to **those** who **love** him. Let no **one say** when he is tempted, "I am **being** tempted by God," for God **cannot** be tempted with **evil**, and he **himself tempts** no one. But **each** person is tempted when he is **lured** and **enticed** by his **own** desire. Then desire when it has conceived **gives birth** to **sin**, and sin when it is **fully** grown **brings forth death**. Do not be deceived, my beloved brothers. **Every** good **gift** and every **perfect** gift is **from above**, **coming** down from the Father of **lights** with **whom there** is no variation or shadow **due** to **change**. (ESV)

```
K P Q Q Z P A R E D N U K K
Z X D W A Q H G G A L U R Z
A S A L L X T C N W C D O G
C L B U I K A G A I M H Z I
S U O H G W E N H N M O R F
O G V U H Y D I C C N O H T
M E E N T I C E D S I O C W
S U Y A S M V B S H F H T M
D K T M A E K W G S L C W P
M D H T R O F S T H E R E N
T K O Y L L U F G F S L L I
F S S O H Z D S R N M A B V
O N E S T P M E T L I V E L
B W A T R S P V R R H R E O
M O D E I O F I T U N Y B V
Y C A N B H I G W A L I F E
```

Solution on Page 344

Love God and Your Neighbor

The Gospel of Mark 12:28–33

One of the scribes **came** up and **heard** them **disputing** with one another, and **seeing** that he **answered** them **well**, **asked** him, "Which commandment is the **most** **important** of **all**?" **Jesus** answered, "The most important is, 'Hear, O **Israel**: The **Lord** our **God**, the Lord is one. And you shall **love** the Lord **your** God with all your heart and with all your **soul** and with all your **mind** and with all your **strength**.' The second is this: 'You shall love your **neighbor** as yourself.' There is no **other** commandment **greater** than these." And the **scribe** **said** to him, "You are **right**, **Teacher**. You have **truly** said that he is one, and there is no other **besides** him. And to love him with all the heart and with all the understanding and with all the strength, and to love one's neighbor as oneself." (ESV)

```
O D M N Y R Y O U R I G H T
I A L L D G S I T W S V N A
A F E R L E N M C Q V A H J
J H A O D S Q I A U T S O M
H E R I N I N N E R R Q S S
H D S B I V S D O E N U T Q
M E I J M W E P H G S S L S
B X V S E K M C U E N T C O
Y W R R S I A A J T E R U U
G R E A T E R L F O I E Z L
N D H L T R U L Y B G N N M
X P T D L T H G E L H G G O
C D O R L S H M M L B T N B
X G I M H P A M L H O H T M
L N M L Y C D I T C R V A U
W I A Y S Z G J D P J E E A
```

Solution on Page 344

Striving after Wind

Ecclesiastes 1:12–17

I the **Preacher** have been **king over Israel** in Jerusalem. And I **applied** my **heart** to **seek** and to **search out** by **wisdom all** that is **done under** heaven. It is an **unhappy** business that **God** has **given** to the **children** of **man** to be **busy** with. I have seen **everything** that is done under the **sun**, and **behold**, all is **vanity** and a **striving after wind**. **What** is **crooked cannot** be made **straight**, and what is lacking cannot be counted. I **said** in my heart, "I have **acquired great** wisdom, surpassing all who were over Jerusalem **before** me, and my heart has had great **experience** of wisdom and knowledge." And I applied my heart to **know** wisdom and to know madness and **folly**. I **perceived** that this also is but a striving after wind. (ESV)

```
X T B Z H D F M O D S I W H
T A E R G O D W T T D S C Q
B H H B B E F O R E T R W S
I W O N K Z N E K R A A E B
T L L A W N T O I E G E M U
G D D U A F O V S G K L I S
S I E C A R I U N H A P P Y
A A V E C N E I R E P X E L
M S I E G C H I L D R E N L
N W E Y N T D O N E E S U O
D I C N Y A Y C V I H C N F
W N R R K T M O A L C U D H
L D E R I U Q C A P A R E X
V V P N N O C R G P E A R W
E H A U G T H G I A R T S O
U V W S B D K K R T P K X B
```

Solution on Page 344

True Riches

The Gospel of Matthew 6:19–24

Lay not up for yourselves treasures upon earth, **where** moth and **rust** doth **corrupt**, and where thieves **break** through and **steal**: But lay up for yourselves treasures in **heaven**, where neither moth **nor** rust doth corrupt, and where thieves do not break through nor steal: For where **your** **treasure** is, there will your heart be **also**. The **light** of the **body** is the **eye**: if therefore thine eye be **single**, **thy** whole body **shall** be **full** of light. But if thine eye be **evil**, thy whole body shall be full of **darkness**. If therefore the light that is in thee be darkness, how **great** is that darkness! No **man** **can** **serve** **two** masters: for either he will **hate** the **one**, and **love** the other; or **else** he will **hold** to the one, and **despise** the other. Ye cannot serve **God** and mammon. (KJV)

```
O D W R G D N Z Q X L V N D
U R D B K X V M M F B K C O
G B D G H L Y W S L U V Y X
Y O U R E R V Y M W H H V L
G D N T E M A N H A T E V R
X Y A E C L A E T S J W C G
Z H M R N O R V U A B K O H
S G B H K E R R B E E V T P
H E A V E N S R A R S R H X
A E S I P S E D U T W O G D
L L U F E A I S H P L S I I
L W M Z K C A N S D T A L U
O A V J E E A L G E S L E G
V P Q N R V A E S L R I H E
E C E T V U D S F O E V Y M
M D U Y Y X P E O C T E E Z
```

Solution on Page 344

A Lame Man Walks

Acts 3:2–8

And a **man lame from birth** was **being carried**, **whom** they **laid daily** at the **gate** of the **temple** that is **called** the Beautiful Gate to **ask alms** of **those** entering the temple. **Seeing Peter** and **John about** to go **into** the temple, he asked to receive alms. And Peter directed his **gaze** at him, as **did** John, and **said**, "Look at us." And he **fixed** his attention on them, expecting to receive something from them. But Peter said, "I have no **silver** and gold, but **what** I do have I **give** to you. In the **name** of **Jesus** Christ of Nazareth, **rise** up and **walk**!" And he **took** him by the **right hand** and **raised** him up, and immediately his **feet** and **ankles** were made **strong**. And leaping up he stood and **began** to walk, and entered the temple with them, walking and leaping and praising **God**. (ESV)

```
M L U B L B S Y Q R E G M D
Q F S X L A I D R T N H O J
W R D R G D L B E I T G H P
R Y M A A S E M E D S A W I
X O T S I I P E S S R E H A
K E T K N L S T S I O A T W
Y N Y G E V Y E G U N H F L
F R O M F E A H D D S R T A
R T E B I R T H D E O E E G
R U Z T X J N V L I L T J S
R T A O E F G K T R D L N W
X H G O D P N U L R T B A I
N U O K D A O B L A M E G C
D A W L I B R G Y C W I E D
M Z W N A M T K V F V U B F
I L S H S N S J C E M A N W
```

Solution on Page 345

The Son Is Heir

Hebrews 1:1–5

Long ago, at **many times** and in many **ways**, God **spoke** to our fathers by the prophets, but in **these last days** he has spoken to us by his **Son**, **whom** he appointed the **heir** of **all things**, **through** whom also he **created** the world. He is the radiance of the **glory** of God and the **exact imprint** of his **nature**, and he **upholds** the universe by the **word** of his **power**. **After making** purification for **sins**, he **sat down** at the **right hand** of the **Majesty** on **high**, **having become** as **much** superior to **angels** as the **name** he has inherited is more excellent than theirs. For to **which** of the angels **did** God **ever** say, "You are my Son, today I have begotten you"? Or again, "I will be to him a father, and he shall be to me a son"? (ESV)

```
S I N S U B L G Y M D R X K
M Y M L A H O O T H E I R B
R M U P M A E R S V K C D Z
G D H F R V F H E R R N H P
A Y T W H I C H J E X A C T
Q U E M A N N W A Y S T U T
Q L O Y B G N T M N H U M H
R H L V N E E H C N G R G I
W O S I W D C R W S R E J N
S S K O S D L O H P U W L G
E A R F N A D U M J T O N S
M D F T E Y Z G H E H P M P
I F N T S S N H L G G A O O
T D E A E A H A F O I N H K
Z E B S H R L P M G R H O E
L M H Z T U O L Y A K Y F L
```

Solution on Page 345

One Mightier Than I Cometh

The Gospel of Luke 3:15–20

And as the **people** were in expectation, and **all men mused** in **their hearts** of **John**, whether he were the **Christ**, or not; John answered, **saying unto** them all, I **indeed baptize** you with **water**; but **one** mightier than I cometh, the **latchet** of **whose shoes** I am not **worthy** to unloose: he shall baptize you with the **Holy Ghost** and with **fire**: Whose **fan** is in his **hand**, and he will thoroughly **purge** his **floor**, and will gather the **wheat into** his **garner**; but the **chaff** he will **burn** with fire unquenchable. And **many** other **things** in his exhortation preached he unto the people. But **Herod** the tetrarch, **being** reproved by him for Herodias his brother Philip's **wife**, and for all the **evils which** Herod had done, **Added** yet this **above** all, that he **shut** up John in prison. (KJV)

```
J F Z W L X K S H U T J C U
I C L F T K H G C H A F F J
D D U N T O E N H B N A L O
W O E M E N Q M O O Y L O H
I R A S N R E V I L S L O N
F E D X U P E O P L E T R A
E H D F H M B N R U B Y F F
S O E S Q W P A R L N U D W
O G D A N O O P P A B Q I J
H A N Y R L Z R M T G N N D
W Q A I W T E L T C I E D B
O W H N H T S I R H C Z E J
M I P G E T F I R E Y I E W
B O M Q A G E N G T N N D Z
B I N L T H P U R G E T W Z
Z E R E T A W H I C H O B J
```

Solution on Page 345

Make Me to Know Your Ways

Psalms 25:1–8

To you, O **LORD**, I **lift** up my **soul**. O my **God**, in you I **trust**; let me not be put to **shame**; let not my **enemies** **exult** over me. **Indeed**, **none** who wait for you shall be put to shame; they shall be ashamed who are wantonly treacherous. **Make** me to **know** **your** ways, O LORD; **teach** me your **paths**. **Lead** me in your truth and teach me, for you are the God of my salvation; for you I wait **all** the **day** **long**. **Remember** your **mercy**, O LORD, and your steadfast **love**, for they have been **from** of **old**. Remember not the **sins** of my youth or my transgressions; **according** to your steadfast love remember me, for the **sake** of your goodness, O LORD! Good and **upright** is the LORD; **therefore** he instructs sinners in the **way**. (ESV)

```
J K D K S M J S N E Y S A Q
D D W H E V O L H A Y W B K
R S T R I E J U D A E L Q O
O A C G M N W P W G M O M G
P Y L A E O R R N Z O E F Q
R B K K N N G I T X X J R S
V E A K E D D G Z U B H R Y
G S L X R R I H L O N G B R
H V A E O E G T I E A H N S
R T C C F B O N R G Q L N V
G E C X E M D B E U V I L E
X A F N R E O R Q S S F N G
J C O J E M R R O U D T H V
O H A D H E P U F L A S E Q
Q D J S T R L K O P L M D G
F J C C F G W O X Y Y F R M
```

Solution on Page 345

She Was Praying

1 Samuel 1:12–18

As she was **praying** to the LORD, **Eli watched** her. Seeing her **lips moving** but hearing no sound, he thought she had been **drinking**. "Must you **come here** drunk?" he demanded. "Throw **away** your **wine**!" "Oh no, sir!" she **replied**. "I haven't been drinking wine or anything **stronger**. But I am **very** discouraged, and I was pouring **out** my heart to the LORD. Don't **think** I am a **wicked** woman! For I have been praying out of great **anguish** and sorrow." "In that case," Eli said, "go in peace! **May** the **God** of Israel **grant** the **request** you have **asked** of him." "Oh, **thank** you, sir!" she **exclaimed**. Then she **went back** and **began** to **eat again**, and she was no **longer sad**. (NLT)

Solution on Page 345

```
D R L P T F H V I R S H Y M
A E T G N I V O M L R D J K
S Q M N K I U Y Y R O L B X
R U D I N T Z R E G N O L C
S E Y K A I H P W P A W O L
S S R N H L L I P S G M N Z
O T E I T I C E N O E N I W
G M V R E K T X R K B G I L
T W F D E A S K E D R Q D H
B U M D D H B T G A P T Z D
J M O P R A Y I N G P Y G E
C G B H C W A T O E O N V H
I D I K W A M A R I W I R C
X B I E D Y U E T H W A N T
I R R D T C P H S I U G N A
I V M W O N J I D E O A J W
```

Solution on Page 346

Advice

Proverbs 25:14–20

A person who **promises** a **gift** but doesn't **give** it is like clouds and **wind** that **bring** no **rain**. Patience **can** persuade a **prince**, and **soft speech** can break **bones**. Do you like **honey**? Don't **eat** too **much**, or it will **make** you **sick**! Don't **visit** your **neighbors** too often, or you will wear **out** your **welcome**. Telling **lies** about **others** is as **harmful** as **hitting** them with an ax, wounding them with a **sword**, or **shooting** them with a **sharp arrow**. Putting confidence in an unreliable person in **times** of trouble is like chewing with a **broken tooth** or **walking** on a **lame foot**. Singing **cheerful songs** to a person with a heavy heart is like **taking** someone's **coat** in **cold** weather or pouring **vinegar** in a wound. (NLT)

```
D R O W S O N G S I U U K B
G S H V N M B O N E S M R L
S N A A R A G E N I V O T M
E R I T R Y E N O H K O X A
I M O R N M C X I E O L K K
L O O B B K F L N T L G A E
F W X N H B R U H I T N V W
J D H C S G P F L S G I F T
S Z U L N R I R W I G T H C
E M Q I A T A E O V X O N O
M R K H L A M E N M U O T L
I A S B T O F H C T I H A D
T I J A C F U C A N E S N O
B N O L B Q O W E R I I E J
H C E E P S N S S C W R N S
B W O C G U C Y K T X F P X
```

Solution on Page 346

Many Rooms

The Gospel of John 14:1–7

"Let not **your** **hearts** be **troubled**. **Believe** in **God**; believe **also** in me. In my **Father**'s **house** are many **rooms**. If it were not so, **would** I have **told** you that I go to **prepare** a **place** for you? And if I go and prepare a place for you, I will **come** **again** and will **take** you to **myself**, that **where** I am you **may** be also. And you **know** the **way** to where I am going." Thomas **said** to him, "Lord, we do not know where you are going. How **can** we know the way?" **Jesus** said to him, "I am the way, and the **truth**, and the **life**. No **one** comes to the Father **except** **through** me. If you had known me, you would have known my Father also. **From** now on you do know him and have **seen** him." (ESV)

Solution on Page 348

```
E D X Y Y I D L O T R U T H
B B W B L N U M L I N Y E Y
W O K U T H E R E H T A F G
X I J D J F E T E H R M C S
J L D S O T B R R T Q I N U
I E N I A G A O S N H B G S
V P F K V P U U T P E C X E
I B E Z E G N B P L S E F J
Q W J R H M J L I N U R S M
H F P O C Y P E R O O M S V
I M F N L S V D G M H S J J
R C Q E R E H W L T Z J L G
N O S U C L S A X U E P K A
S B O A D F I Y E M O C Q J
M Y L C I V P F K N O W K E
G P G T S D X G E E Z W M Y
```

Solution on Page 346

Crowds Follow Jesus

The Gospel of Mark 3:7–12

But **Jesus** withdrew himself with his disciples to the **sea**: and a **great** multitude **from Galilee** followed him, and from **Judaea**, And from Jerusalem, and from **Idumaea**, and from **beyond Jordan**; and they **about Tyre** and **Sidon**, a great multitude, when they had heard **what** great **things** he **did**, **came unto** him. And he **spake** to his disciples, that a **small ship should wait** on him because of the multitude, **lest** they should **throng** him. For he had **healed many**; insomuch that they pressed **upon** him for to **touch** him, as many as had **plagues**. And unclean spirits, when they **saw** him, **fell down before** him, and **cried**, saying, **Thou art** the **Son** of **God**. And he straitly charged them that they should not **make** him **known**. (KJV)

```
T N Y S N F J W H U T V E K
G H E W U O A B K Z X K C O
D S O P J S M A L L J F H I
X N O U D P E M A C C N E Y
K N O S A E D J A G P C K X
S Y D Y E E I O U K J K F F
P H N E E U A R W J E F E S
A G O U L B G D C N E R T A
K O D U I A A A U L K J Y R
E D I D L E E N L J Q Y Z T
B T S S A D R H T P O T K A
E C I M G S M O R F B T E H
S C U A O N U Y F T S S N W
H D S N W C I T A E R G V U
I V Z Y H X Z H L A B O U T
P C R J W F X I T H R O N G
```

Solution on Page 346

Living Stone

1 Peter 2:4–8

You are coming to **Christ**, the **living stone** who was **rejected** by **humans** but was **chosen** as **precious** by **God**. You **come** to him as living stones, a **spiritual house** that is **being built into** a **holy** priesthood. So **offer** spiritual sacrifices that God **accepts through Jesus** Christ. That is why **Scripture says**, "I am **laying** a chosen and precious cornerstone in **Zion**, and the **person** who believes in him will **never** be ashamed." This **honor belongs** to **those** who **believe**. But to those who don't believe: "The stone that the builders rejected has become the cornerstone, a stone that **people trip over**, a **large rock** that people **find** offensive." The people tripped over the **word because** they **refused** to believe it. **Therefore**, this is how they **ended** up. (GW)

```
O V E R O N O H S J R O C K
T H O S E E J R U T Y H L F
T S H G U O R H T M O Y I A
Y N S N N L E D L S A N Z O
D T V O S I M Y E I D N E T
H D H L S U Y N P S V R S N
B S Y E C T O A P E U I O I
O U I B R Z P I L B R F N W
F S I C I E R E C H D S E G
F E E L P I F M C E R Q O R
E J F S T E T O T C R D C N
R Q T U U U L C R N A P G O
S Y A S R A E P D E D N E I
Y L O H E J C D O V I R A Z
H B I B E L I E V E S U O H
U E G R A L X G B R P I R T
```

Solution on Page 347

On a White Horse

Revelation 19:11–15

Then I **saw** heaven **opened**, and **behold**, a white **horse**! The **one** sitting on it is **called** Faithful and **True**, and in righteousness he **judges** and **makes war**. His **eyes** are like a **flame** of **fire**, and on his **head** are **many diadems**, and he has a **name** written that no one **knows** but **himself**. He is **clothed** in a robe **dipped** in **blood**, and the name by **which** he is called is The **Word** of **God**. And the **armies** of heaven, **arrayed** in **fine linen**, white and **pure**, were following him on white horses. From his **mouth comes** a **sharp** sword with which to **strike down** the nations, and he will **rule** them with a **rod** of iron. He will **tread** the winepress of the **fury** of the **wrath** of God the Almighty. (ESV)

Solution on Page 347

```
J M S W H I C H M A F Q M Q
H S L B W E L A O F J N W X
F E H S S J N N U R W A R X
A M T E S Y A R T J S S I O
Q A A K N M Y R H T R E A D
H L R A E X U D R R K Y E B
L F W M N E V I R F N E R J
U Y E K I J K B L O O D U O
G O D C L E U E I S W A P Y
Q E T L O B S D M R S E E S
V L T O O M R E G D N H R F
Z U E T I H D O D E P P I D
P R A H S A E I D L S N F O
O N E E I S F B H L E U E W
N A Y D E Y A R R A C M B N
D O P A X D P H R C O M E S
```

Solution on Page 347

Pay Attention!

Acts 20:28–32

"**Pay** attention to yourselves and to the **entire flock** in **which** the **Holy Spirit** has **placed** you as **bishops** to be shepherds for **God**'s **church** which he acquired with his **own blood**. I know that **fierce wolves** will come to you **after** I **leave**, and they won't spare the flock. Some of **your** own **men** will come **forward** and **say things** that **distort** the **truth**. They will do this to **lure** disciples **into** following them. So be alert! Remember that I instructed **each** of you for **three years**, **day** and **night**, at times with **tears** in my **eyes**. I am now entrusting you to God and to his message that **tells** how **kind** he is. That message **can help** you grow and can **give** you the inheritance that is **shared** by **all** of God's holy **people**." (GW)

```
H S E V L O W H Z V B G Y Z
I C P B S H A R E D N I K E
B X A I J S G N I H T U R T
A F T E R V T E L L S W K E
D R J J T I T H E S X E V F
U S B J R Q T C G O V S E N
P K B E O T N I Y I R B C S
K L M I T M E H G A N L L A
M C E Q S A M W E H X O N Y
E H Y H I H C T C C N O D K
U A E G D F O R W A R D P C
P T S L F E U P C H E E V O
T H R E E H G B S C O V I L
G T A U C A R J A P W L U F
O Y E W O R V L L N N R Y P
D A Y N Q Y P E K I E V A G
```

Solution on Page 347

The Four Chariots

Zechariah 6:2–8

The **first** **chariot** had **red** **horses**. The **second** had **black** horses. The **third** had **white** horses. And the fourth had **strong**, **spotted** horses. I **asked** the **angel** who was **speaking** with me, "What do **these** horses **mean**, sir?" The angel answered, "They are the four spirits of **heaven**. They are **going** **out** **after** **standing** in the presence of the **Lord** of the **whole** **earth**. The chariot with the black horses is going **toward** the **north**, and the white horses are **following** them. The spotted **ones** are going toward the south." When these strong horses **went** out, they were **eager** to **patrol** the earth. He **said**, "Go, patrol the earth!" And they patrolled the earth. Then he **called** out to me, "Look! **Those** who went to the north have **made** my **Spirit** rest in the north." (GW)

```
D O H X B R C J X L S K C B
A M O M B E S E H T Y P B D
O V R I E G D S P I R I T F
S N S Z D A N G A G E D T M
Z L E P G E N C T D S U V B
D Q S S V I Y I R P O N C W
N K P A D D S A O E H P L E
O I E N E A W T L H T R O N
C H A R I O T S R I F F J T
E T K D T E X G W O F A A R
S A I P D K C A L B N N S M
C O N G N R T A E R H G K L
K Z G N I W O L L O F E E A
K W H I T E O L C L C L C L D T
K U V O G H H H T R A E A A N
F R W G W B H T H I R D M X
```

Solution on Page 347

Commanded to Love

2 John 1:5–9

I am **writing** to **remind** you, **dear friends**, that we should **love** one **another**. This is not a **new** commandment, but one we have had **from** the beginning. Love **means doing what God** has commanded us, and he has commanded us to love one another, **just** as you **heard** from the beginning. I **say** this **because many** deceivers have gone **out into** the **world**. They **deny** that **Jesus Christ came** in a **real body**. **Such** a person is a deceiver and an antichrist. **Watch** out that you do not **lose** what we have worked so **hard** to **achieve**. Be diligent so that you **receive** your **full reward**. Anyone who **wanders away** from this teaching has no relationship with God. But anyone who **remains** in the teaching of Christ has a relationship with **both** the **Father** and the **Son**. (NLT)

```
C I C A C H I E V E R X X E
F R I E N D S R D R K K S M
S H G T O O R A E J H U U A
L O N I B M T H Y M A D S C
F H N E Y J T H R C I E E C
G G T R W A N D E R S N J Y
W M R O F O N B M R H Y D G
H B R R B U D R A E H O N L
P L O H T T L Y I C B I A Z
D M X T C S Q L N E T E Q V
G O A U N U U T S I R H C M
O N G N W I S O R V Y W E V
G D L E Y U L W R E W A R D
H A D Y J O D A N A N T W A
G A T N V L E X T S S C O A
M N M E H D R A H F W H A T
```

Solution on Page 348

Faith Comes from Hearing

Romans 10:17–21

So **faith** **comes** **from** hearing, and hearing through the **word** of **Christ**. But I **ask**, have they not heard? **Indeed** they have, for "**Their** **voice** has **gone** **out** to **all** the **earth**, and their words to the **ends** of the world." But I ask, **did** **Israel** not **understand**? **First** **Moses** says, "I will **make** you jealous of **those** who are not a **nation**; with a **foolish** nation I will make you angry." Then Isaiah is so **bold** as to **say**, "I have been found by those who did not **seek** me; I have **shown** **myself** to those who did not ask for me." But of Israel he says, "All **day** **long** I have **held** out my **hands** to a disobedient and **contrary** people." (ESV)

Solution on Page 348

```
D U F M Y C L L E G U L J S
Q U P Y A D Y T H O S E D C
K U H Z S S L S D N E A N M
U M B I G B S E E K C R A Q
C Q K U Y W O C H R I S T H
D X F M O E S L A N O I S Y
S I L R A H F E D L V I R X
L O D S O K L E M X L A E C
T O D W Z M E T H O R S D Q
G O N E N D S Q O T C D N U
R W I G V R Y F N U R N U O
U W H X I L M O A K F A S F
F O B F H M C S T A D H E D
Q J S Q I J K R I E H T S B
W L C Z K O U T O M V P O A
Q K J U W B H N N L O S M U
```

Solution on Page 348

Imperishable Beauty

1 Peter 3:1–6

Likewise, **wives**, be **subject** to **your** **own** husbands, so that **even** if **some** do not **obey** the word, they **may** be **won** **without** a word by the **conduct** of **their** wives, when they **see** your respectful and **pure** conduct. Do not let your adorning be external—the **braiding** of **hair** and the **putting** on of gold **jewelry**, or the **clothing** you wear—but let your adorning be the **hidden** **person** of the **heart** with the imperishable **beauty** of a **gentle** and **quiet** **spirit**, **which** in **God**'s **sight** is **very** precious. For this is how the **holy** women who **hoped** in God used to **adorn** themselves, by submitting to their own husbands, as **Sarah** obeyed **Abraham**, **calling** him **lord**. And you are her **children**, if you do good and do not **fear** **anything** that is frightening. (ESV)

```
Y Q G N B M E H J N E Y T H
R X S C K W E A C W H O M H
E R U P H A S O B O B U A A
V G B D R I N C L R R R Y B
C P J T R D L Y T U A E B T
A E E M U O B D T S I H H Q
T R C C T G L H R H D G A B
Z S T H O U O H I E I K F M
K O I J B P O Y E S N N O W
F N E V E N G H H Y G S G I
G O D D Y W S N T N P I R V
X K E L T N E G I I O T Z E
U F E A R D R L R T W E K S
F U E O D I L I R I T I K O
G K D I A A T W E Y D U F M
F A H H C I H W A T V Q P E
```

Solution on Page 348

Show the Truth by Action

1 John 3:14–18

If we **love** our Christian brothers and sisters, it **proves** that we have **passed** **from** death to **life**. But a **person** who has no love is **still** **dead**. **Anyone** who hates another brother or **sister** is really a **murderer** at **heart**. And you **know** that murderers don't have **eternal** life **within** them. We know **what** **real** love is because **Jesus** **gave** up his life for us. So we **also** **ought** to **give** up our lives for our brothers and sisters. If **someone** has enough **money** to **live** **well** and **sees** a brother or sister in **need** but shows no compassion—how **can** God's love be in that person? Dear **children**, let's not **merely** **say** that we love **each** **other**; let us **show** the **truth** by our **actions**. (NLT)

```
S Z E C E S N E M D N P B T
A H V H H T F T U L F W L O
Y H O B G I V E R F L S C B
S W L W L L L P D A A E T N
D H X I K L A D E E E T W Z
O A T B V S P N R T R H R H
E T R U S E O R E E S G U L
U Y L E R E M N R R N U T Q
C M D S M T O C A N O O W Z
T O O O I Y W H H A I I O Y
P N S O N S V C M L T L N X
J E E A J U T A J H C E K F
D Y V M N S I E I D A E D X
C I O T H E R N R Q L V A S
V R R E Z J E S E E S A A N
F K P E U K S D M V O G C Q
```

Solution on Page 348

Speak Wisely

Proverbs 15:1–9

A **gentle** **answer** **deflects** **anger**, but **harsh** **words** **make** **tempers** **flare**. The **tongue** of the **wise** makes knowledge appealing, but the mouth of a **fool** **belches** **out** foolishness. The LORD is watching everywhere, keeping his **eye** on **both** the **evil** and the **good**. Gentle words are a **tree** of **life**; a deceitful tongue **crushes** the **spirit**. Only a fool **despises** a parent's discipline; whoever **learns** **from** correction is wise. There is treasure in the house of the **godly**, but the earnings of the **wicked** **bring** trouble. The **lips** of the wise **give** good **advice**; the **heart** of a fool has **none** to give. The LORD detests the sacrifice of the wicked, but he **delights** in the **prayers** of the **upright**. The LORD detests the **way** of the wicked, but he **loves** **those** who **pursue** godliness. (NLT)

```
E S I W X E F I L E P F B J
T E T K W G I V E U S O O C
H U E C K O D C A S T O T F
Z L O V E S R Z R R R X L H L
P I G O D L Y D N U D S W T
E V K U M T F Y S P S E Y E
F E A O O I D E L I G H T S
L L N N H R C E D T W C E G
A V G B R I N G S K U L T S
R U E W V V P H R F P W E E O
E H R D A S E S R G I B M L
E K A M R Y Z I E T C S P V
H V Y A A M G N W R K D E F
C C H R S H T S S E E O R S
L I P S T L N O N E D O S P
Z S X H E A R T A V M G H H
```

Solution on Page 349

A Faithful Centurion

The Gospel of Matthew 8:8–12

But the centurion **replied**, "Lord, I am not worthy to have you **come** under my **roof**, but only **say** the **word**, and my **servant** will be healed. For I too am a **man** under authority, with **soldiers** under me. And I say to **one**, 'Go,' and he **goes**, and to **another**, 'Come,' and he comes, and to my servant, 'Do this,' and he does it." When **Jesus heard** this, he marveled and said to **those** who **followed** him, "Truly, I **tell** you, with no one in **Israel** have I **found such faith**. I tell you, many will come **from east** and **west** and **recline** at **table** with **Abraham**, Isaac, and **Jacob** in the **kingdom** of heaven, **while** the sons of the kingdom will be **thrown into** the **outer** darkness." (ESV)

```
A W B O C A J F E T V S O N
Y B D Z P D N E U D Z E F J
A S R E I D L O S H R L Q P
M U T A W I O U T E R O O F
B S A Y H O J B N H R N W B
I E E W N A L A L T E A S T
A J B O G W M L Q I C R B T
W K F F G Y O R O A L I T R
Z I N T O R D R T F I S H A
F R N H X U G B H V N R O I
O V Z S J U N V P T E A S F
M D H C P M I D P P H E E T
N K F C O W K L L E T L V H
P A G R U M E I A U B S A P
O J F W F S E R V A N T E V
K B L G I D D L T E Y T O W
```

Solution on Page 349

Daniel in the Lions' Den

Daniel 6:16–20

So at **last** the **king gave** orders for **Daniel** to be **arrested** and thrown **into** the **den** of lions. The king **said** to him, "May your **God**, **whom** you **serve** so **faithfully**, **rescue** you." A stone was brought and **placed over** the mouth of the den. The king sealed the stone with his **own** royal seal and the seals of his **nobles**, so that no **one** could rescue Daniel. Then the king **returned** to his palace and **spent** the **night fasting**. He **refused** his usual entertainment and couldn't **sleep** at **all** that night. Very **early** the **next morning**, the king got up and **hurried out** to the lions' den. When he got **there**, he called out in **anguish**, "Daniel, servant of the **living** God! Was your God, whom you serve so faithfully, **able** to rescue you **from** the lions?" (NLT)

```
A J L T P L G T V M W X F O
I E J L L G O G P H M S B H
J S B A A J E W O C B N T Z
R P O S C T Y M N D X G Z H
N E X T E V W J E S X P K V
V N V L D L E S T S E W S A
W T B O U V B O Y G L Y R R
G A H C A V T O Y A L E E R
N G V G V N Z D N L T F E G
I N G N I K A G U U U S N P
T I E Z F N U F R S C I E O
S N A F I I H N E U V V Y T
A R R E S T E D E I R R U H
F O L H I D U D L E G Z Y E
M M Y A P M R O S A I D E R
H O F P G E P U G G V G O E
```

Solution on Page 349

You Must Be Born Again

The Gospel of John 3:3–8

Jesus replied, "I **tell** you the **truth**, **unless** you are **born** again, you cannot **see** the **Kingdom** of **God**." "What do you mean?" **exclaimed** **Nicodemus**. "How **can** an **old** **man** go **back** **into** his mother's **womb** and be born again?" Jesus replied, "I **assure** you, no **one** can **enter** the Kingdom of God **without** **being** born of **water** and the **Spirit**. Humans can **reproduce** only human **life**, but the Holy Spirit **gives** **birth** to spiritual life. So don't be surprised when I **say**, 'You must be born again.' The **wind** **blows** wherever it **wants**. **Just** as you can **hear** the wind but can't tell **where** it **comes** **from** or where it is going, so you can't **explain** how **people** are born of the Spirit." (NLT)

```
J I L Z F U R U R Z K R R B
P Q S Q V D N M O S X E E J
O F E G E P J D O G P T T S
O V E G S J V T W R H N A W
Q U B X Z U N C O K F E W E
I R N N P I M D L E O K A N
D P A L S L U E J L I F E R
K M C W E C A M D P E O L G
C C O M E S S I D O N T Y M
A L T J N P S A N E C W K C
B H T R I B U L I P H I T Y
S E O R U W R C W E N U N X
P B I Q A T E X R G I V E S
K T Z N O V H E D L D J R A
W I T O G T U O H T I W U Y
T S U J W O M B B Z F I N C
```

Solution on Page 349

Creation Waits

Romans 8:18–23

I consider our present **sufferings** insignificant **compared** to the **glory** that will soon be revealed to us. **All** creation is **eagerly** waiting for **God** to reveal who his **children** are. Creation was **subjected** to frustration but not by its **own choice**. The **one** who subjected it to frustration **did** so in the **hope** that it **would** also be **set free from slavery** to **decay** in **order** to **share** the glorious freedom that the children of God will have. We know that all creation has been groaning with the **pains** of **childbirth** up to the present **time**. However, not only creation groans. We, who have the **Spirit** as the **first** of God's **gifts**, also **groan inwardly**. We groan as we eagerly **wait** for our adoption, the freeing of our bodies from **sin**. (GW)

```
W Y L D G W C C F S M I X J
A L A C O R D E R Q R Y Q W
C T Z U R G O N O C C C V D
R N L Y N L L A M H H Q A I
Y D Y L D R A W N I O W N T
S L A V E R Y Z L L I Z I E
P G R C A W E D D D C M Z S
I X N E A T B E E R E Y M B
R O V I G I R U T E N F I O
I G T L R A E N C N J L R Q
T S O T P E E D E C A Y U J
P R H M R A F P J B B W N P
Y O O F R I I F B N H J Z O
A C P G R D V N U I E J X N
C L E S G I F T S S H A R E
R U T Q Y D O C Z D C D C P
```

Solution on Page 350

Faith More Precious Than Gold

1 Peter 1:3–7

God has given us a **new birth because** of his **great mercy**. We have been **born into** a new **life** that has a confidence **which** is **alive** because **Jesus Christ** has **come back** to life. We have been born into a new life which has an inheritance that can't be destroyed or corrupted and can't **fade away**. That inheritance is **kept** in heaven for you, **since** you are **guarded** by God's **power** through **faith** for a salvation that is ready to be revealed at the **end** of **time**. You are extremely **happy about these things**, even **though** you have to **suffer** different **kinds** of trouble for a **little** while now. The **purpose** of these troubles is to **test your** faith as **fire** tests how genuine gold is. Your faith is more precious than gold, and by passing the test, it **gives praise**, **glory**, and **honor** to God. (GW)

```
T R E S E H T E S T M W T G
J R A R Y C Q L P L S G Q N
Y L I A P X N Q L T I R H S
F F W E S G N I H T E F U S
C A K J I N T O S W G F E Q
E M I T B T U D O W F S G P
X W N T L G S P J E O R O E
U E D E H Y T I R P E N D M
W T S J W D E D R A U G E O
E J Y M H V H U T H I R S C
E N P T I H P O T R C S J O
K Z P L C T R R N Y C T E C
E D A F H P I C Y O U R S E
P E H Y N B H G L O R Y U D
T J O P O K C A B O R N S H
S J D V B E C A U S E V I G
```

Solution on Page 350

Peter Speaks

Acts 4:8–12

Then **Peter**, because he was **filled** with the **Holy Spirit**, **said** to them, "Rulers and **leaders** of the **people**, today you are cross-examining us **about** the good we **did** for a **crippled man**. You **want** to **know** how he was made **well**. You and **all** the people of **Israel must** understand that this man **stands** in **your presence** with a healthy **body** because of the **power** of **Jesus Christ from Nazareth**. You crucified Jesus Christ, but **God** has **brought** him **back** to **life**. He is the stone that the **builders rejected**, the stone that has **become** the cornerstone. No **one else can save** us. **Indeed**, we can be saved only by the power of the one **named** Jesus and not by any **other** person." (GW)

```
M U S T Q W S R P N K N V Z
W O B A P V W R R E N U R T
A W R E J E C T E D O G Y A
B G T F I M A N S D W P X Z
Y E P W Q S A A E V A S L R
R O R V S Z R W N E S E Y E
S P U B A C K A C R T M L W
K Z C R I P P L E D A O O O
I T E V R D I D U L N C H P
Y T H D E L L I F P D E W W
H S Y G T I R S N S S B E O
J I E D U L E A P D J A L N
X R T B O O L I F E E S L E
O H B A B B R D T M S E B L
X C A N A I U B U A U S D R
P G W O T H E R Z N S E X D
```

Solution on Page 350

The Good Shepherd

The Gospel of John 10:11–16

"I am the **good** shepherd. The good shepherd sacrifices his **life** for the **sheep**. A **hired hand** will **run** when he **sees** a **wolf coming**. He will abandon the sheep **because** they don't belong to him and he isn't their shepherd. And so the wolf **attacks** them and **scatters** the **flock**. The hired hand runs **away** because he's **working** only for the money and doesn't **really care about** the sheep. I am the good shepherd; I know my **own** sheep, and they know me, just as my Father knows me and I know the Father. So I **sacrifice** my life for the sheep. I have **other** sheep, too, that are not in this sheepfold. I **must bring** them **also**. They will **listen** to my **voice**, and there will be **one** flock with one shepherd." (NLT)

```
S A C R I F I C E D R G G W
B C B R I N G D H N N T I T
E U A O W N E T S I L A P T
Q J E T U T S U M C R L H Y
N L H H T T G O O D Y E I Y
T Z X E B E C A U S E A D L
U X V R W O R K I N G Y W L
E X M U D K K S K C A T T A
J B P V N O Q H G C V L G E
D Z Z A M P N E F L O W S R
X P C R I S U E Q Y I L N O
Z Z I A J S R P P O C Q F C
Y U A U G H F S Z A E Y S T
Q F U N H A R E R I M F V F
J N M J E I Y E G Q Y N I Z
P B C L P P G S G P R L M L
```

Solution on Page 350

Dreams and Visions

Joel 2:28–32

"And it shall come to **pass afterward**, that I will pour **out** my **Spirit** on **all flesh**; your **sons** and your daughters shall **prophesy**, your **old men** shall **dream** dreams, and your young men shall **see visions**. Even on the male and female servants in those days I will pour out my Spirit. And I will show wonders in the **heavens** and on the **earth**, **blood** and **fire** and columns of smoke. The **sun** shall be **turned** to darkness, and the **moon** to blood, before the **great** and awesome **day** of the LORD comes. And it shall come to pass that everyone who calls on the name of the LORD shall be saved. For in Mount **Zion** and in Jerusalem **there** shall be those who **escape**, as the LORD has **said**, and among the survivors shall be those **whom** the LORD calls." (ESV)

```
N B N J F B M V B K J E V S
T G U D F Z Y A L C N R E U
H I C L I B H T Z H V E W N
B S A O O B A F O F Q H M N
A Z N K Z G L V S O O T E I
J C D O E E O B I M M I P Y
M U I R S A X D D M O R A R
G A K H A N R O F H O I C A
U A W P J W O T U P N P S C
R F I R P L R I H T S S E V
H S L J B A Q E S W N M Z C
N I O D I T S S T I E A U F
C H Q Q C Y A S U F V E I O
L X I D N I U E L L A R L D
H F O Q D Y T U R N E D A Y
L O E K F N Q M J G H R W R
```

Solution on Page 351

God Gives Solomon Wisdom

1 Kings 4:29–34

And **God gave Solomon** wisdom and understanding **beyond** measure, and **breadth** of mind like the **sand** on the seashore, so that Solomon's wisdom **surpassed** the wisdom of **all** the **people** of the east and all the wisdom of Egypt. For he was **wiser** than all **other men**, wiser than **Ethan** the **Ezrahite**, and **Heman**, Calcol, and Darda, the **sons** of **Mahol**, and his fame was in all the surrounding **nations**. He also **spoke** 3,000 proverbs, and his songs were 1,005. He spoke of **trees**, **from** the **cedar** that is in **Lebanon** to the **hyssop** that **grows out** of the wall. He spoke also of **beasts**, and of **birds**, and of **reptiles**, and of fish. And people of all nations came to **hear** the wisdom of Solomon, and from all the **kings** of the earth, who had heard of his wisdom. (ESV)

```
Y G E W M W E S S E T J E V
N D A W T H L Z U T L C A S
J E D L Q Y T B R H W S B E
I T H E A R C D P A L L E L
J I D K L H E M A N H K A I
F N N O M O L O S E O I S T
R A H P G Z G L S O R Q T P
O A P S J R H W E K T B S E
M G L B E Y O N D B N H S R
W B W I S E R W G R A D E C
N Z Q S G R K C S B T N P R
C N O E N X Z W F X I E O S
Y P Z E I R I K H D O R O N
S C M R K G T U O P N N D E
Z C G T X R F G L X S A I S
I T X H A H K E V A G B S J
```

Solution on Page 351

The Lord Heals the Brokenhearted

Psalms 147:2–11

The **LORD** **builds** up Jerusalem; he gathers the outcasts of **Israel**. He heals the brokenhearted and **binds** up **their** wounds. He determines the **number** of the **stars**; he **gives** to **all** of them their **names**. **Great** is our Lord, and abundant in **power**; his understanding is **beyond** measure. The LORD **lifts** up the **humble**; he **casts** the wicked to the ground. **Sing** to the LORD with thanksgiving; make **melody** to our **God** on the **lyre**! He **covers** the heavens with **clouds**; he prepares **rain** for the earth; he makes **grass** **grow** on the **hills**. He gives to the **beasts** their **food**, and to the **young** **ravens** that **cry**. His delight is not in the strength of the **horse**, **nor** his pleasure in the **legs** of a **man**, but the LORD **takes** pleasure in **those** who **fear** him, in those who **hope** in his steadfast **love**. (ESV)

```
P C Y O U N G N A T Y R C N
R R F M E R U P A H H A N K
H A E E A M S H O R S E Y U
I O V S B N V P U W D F I E
L S S E T D E M Q M E D S R
L T R S N S B Q Y S B R H Y
S T B A G S A D B B A L B L
E H S R E V O C V T O E E N
E V O L S L J L S V Y B A I
B W T N E F O O D O I M S A
U U O M V L V U N N E D T R
M T W S I N G D D S L A S P
L H R F G O D S G I E E H G
X O T O H L Z E U R K N A D
N S R Y G H L B G A J P C F
M E J D Y S Q A T W M I N Y
```

Solution on Page 351

Spiritual Devotion

2 Thessalonians 2:13–17

We **always** have to **thank God** for you, **brothers** and **sisters**. You are **loved** by the **Lord** and we thank God that in the **beginning** he **chose** you to be saved **through** a **life** of **spiritual devotion** and **faith** in the **truth**. With this in **mind** he **called** you by the Good **News which** we **told** you so that you **would obtain** the glory of our Lord **Jesus Christ**. Then, brothers and sisters, **firmly hold** on to the **traditions** we **taught** you **either** when we **spoke** to you or in our **letter**. God our **Father** loved us and by his **kindness gave** us everlasting encouragement and good **hope**. **Together** with our Lord Jesus Christ, may he **encourage** and **strengthen** you to do and **say everything** that is good. (GW)

```
X D L O T K T A U G H T R F
G A V E B S E H J E S U S S
J N S B R T I N R S A Y D N
Y L I F E G A R U O C N E L
V K S H T G R I H H U H R O
J D T I T R I E N C T G E V
L H E Y E Y S N H G V F H E
D O R L L L R Y N T F D T D
A L S M L O A E A I E O A E
F D P R N A R U V W N G F V
J L O I K T C D T E L G O O
U U K F S N O I T I D A R T
F O E A S R E H T O R B M I
G W H I C H A R E H T I E O
T R U T H N X S W E N B P N
E P O H K F K I N D N E S S
```

Solution on Page 351

Fight the Good Fight

1 Timothy 6:11–16

But as for you, O **man** of **God**, **flee** these **things**. **Pursue** righteousness, godliness, **faith**, **love**, steadfastness, gentleness. **Fight** the good fight of the faith. **Take hold** of the eternal **life** to **which** you were called and **about** which you made the good confession in the presence of many witnesses. I **charge** you in the presence of God, who **gives** life to **all** things, and of **Christ Jesus**, who in his testimony **before** Pontius **Pilate** made the good confession, to **keep** the commandment **unstained** and **free from reproach until** the **appearing** of our **Lord** Jesus Christ, which he will **display** at the **proper** time— he who is the blessed and only **Sovereign**, the **King** of kings and Lord of lords, who alone has immortality, who **dwells** in unapproachable **light**, **whom** no **one** has **ever** seen or **can see**. To him be honor and eternal dominion. **Amen**. (ESV)

```
T Z F C G U G T R V Q A G E
W T E H C I H W D R O L X E
G C T G T I J E S U S L U R
J E N W N P N U N D E S N F
U C V G L I R T L O R N U A
O S S S A D R O S U G C N M
Q E B T W Y H A P I L A T E
E Q S E A Y B T E E R N I N
Q N L F F K A R F P R H L W
U L Z A A O E L R R P N C C
S M I E B V R E P R O A C H
D T E V O L V E P S L M R A
H L F S U E W S E V I G S R
F I G H T H G I L E N D I G
M M W G O D K E F I L H M E
R E U M U G B L K K E S N Y
```

Solution on Page 352

Swing Your Sickle Now

Revelation 14:14–18

Then I **saw** a **white cloud**, and **seated** on the cloud was someone like the Son of **Man**. He had a **gold** crown on his **head** and a **sharp sickle** in his **hand**. Then **another angel came from** the **Temple** and **shouted** to the **one sitting** on the cloud, "Swing the sickle, for the **time** of **harvest** has **come**; the **crop** on **earth** is **ripe**." So the one sitting on the cloud **swung** his sickle **over** the earth, and the **whole** earth was harvested. **After** that, another angel came from the Temple in heaven, and he **also** had a sharp sickle. Then another angel, who had **power** to **destroy** with **fire**, came from the **altar**. He shouted to the angel with the sharp sickle, "Swing **your** sickle now to **gather** the **clusters** of **grapes** from the **vines** of the earth, for they are ripe for judgment." (NLT)

Solution on Page 352

```
L D B E P J E S O G O P M A
L R A T L A V G N V O W G T
R Y O U R P O W E R H L I C
D U F T M R M R C I L M D P
N W H O L E D E T A E S R O
A G R A P E S E T S G G F D
H S B U S R V I H G N U W S
E A U T V F A O C I A J O I
A N R H I S U H T K C S E T
D O G V N T W T S S L M P Z
Y T A G E A I K X A O E I Q
I H T D S S R C Q C U I R F
B E H Z R E T F A I D J I E
S R E T S U L C R M I R N Q
G Y R E B Y T L O O E A O E
S R O M A P I U Z F M H C T
```

Solution on Page 352

A Roman Citizen

Acts 22:25–29

But when the **soldiers** had **Paul** **stretch** **out** to **tie** him to the whipping **post** with the **straps**, Paul **asked** the **sergeant** who was **standing** **there**, "Is it **legal** for you to **whip** a Roman citizen who hasn't had a trial?" When the sergeant **heard** this, he **reported** it to his commanding **officer**. The sergeant asked him, "What are you **doing**? This **man** is a Roman citizen." The officer **went** to Paul and asked him, "Tell me, are you a Roman citizen?" Paul **answered**, "Yes." The officer **replied**, "I **paid** a **lot** of **money** to **become** a Roman citizen." Paul replied, "But I was **born** a Roman citizen." Immediately, the soldiers who were **going** to question Paul **stepped** **away** **from** him. The officer was **afraid** when he found out that he had tied up a Roman citizen. (GW)

Solution on Page 352

```
Q G R L B G L T K S U M I M
V E H T H E R E H A O L H P
Z Q Y E G T C C A N V X P Z
M R P A U L T O E S O D J J
X B L O W E N Y M W K Y B Y
Y A A Y R A A R O E R E Z B
Q F E T G R E P O R T E D P
X A S C N C G T N E W Y K W
F I I T I S R E I D L O S O
Q V B F O T E X P A I D T R
R H F V G A S A F D I F E T
B O R N G N S R S T R A P S
V W B W P D A J T O L A P O
P R E P L I E D M K T I E P
J Z V E D N H A G N I O D H
N C H V D G N W R G R E U I
```

Solution on Page 352

Compassionate and Merciful

James 5:7–11

Be **patient**, **therefore**, **brothers**, **until** the **coming** of the **Lord**. **See** how the **farmer** **waits** for the **precious** **fruit** of the earth, **being** patient **about** it, until it **receives** the **early** and the **late** **rains**. You **also**, be patient. **Establish** **your** hearts, for the coming of the Lord is at **hand**. Do not **grumble** **against** **one** **another**, brothers, so that you **may** not be judged; **behold**, the **Judge** is **standing** at the **door**. As an **example** of **suffering** and patience, brothers, **take** the **prophets** who **spoke** in the **name** of the Lord. Behold, we consider those blessed who remained **steadfast**. You have heard of the steadfastness of **Job**, and you have seen the purpose of the Lord, how the Lord is compassionate and **merciful**. (ESV)

```
T V G N I D N A T S U M M R
R T W L W L G B E H O L D W
P H A I M A Y V O S L A N P
M A I T I T I B B U B A I S
L N T N A E H D O O R Z U T
P O S U C K P E U I J F E E
X T T E P H E T R C F E L H
F H R T S A F D A E T S B P
B E E M R T T A R R F L M O
E R F L E S A I R P Y O U R
I X Y N H R N B E M R R R P
N D T A T G C I L N E D G E
G N I M O C O I A I T R L K
P A U E R S N Q F R S X S O
Y H R D B E E G D U J H S P
L U F F J E X A M P L E P S
```

Solution on Page 352

Jesus Cried Out

The Gospel of Mark 15:33–39

At **noon** darkness **came over** the **whole land until three** in the afternoon. At three o'clock **Jesus cried out** in a loud **voice**, "**Eloi**, Eloi, lema sabachthani?" **which means**, "My **God**, my God, why have you abandoned me?" When some of the **people** standing **there heard** him say that, they said, "Listen! He's **calling Elijah**." Someone **ran** and soaked a **sponge** in vinegar. Then he put it on a **stick** and offered Jesus a **drink**. The **man** said, "Let's **see** if Elijah **comes** to **take** him down." Then Jesus cried out in a loud voice and **died**. The **curtain** in the **temple** was **split** in **two from top** to bottom. When the officer who stood **facing** Jesus **saw** how he **gave** up his **spirit**, he said, "Certainly, this man was the **Son** of God!" (GW)

```
G S H Z M B S G O D K I Y K
A J O M D J L U O V O I C E
C U V N D I C J Z U E I X V
M G A V E E S H E P T R U D
R L S P I G P A E S P L I T
H O G P D E N J N L U D J A
G Z N L O R T I R I P S L K
R Y I P M N A L C E X M D E
Q S L C O T G E R A N P E V
C E L H R K H E H S F A I T
H M A U F C H M E K N I R D
R O C L I T N U M R N A C B
S C W H O L E N A M H M E M
S A W T H M E L C B L T N M
D U A A T L N O O N D O P R
I V H T I Q X Q H I V P W F
```

Solution on Page 353

Clothed in White Robes

Revelation 7:9–13

After this I **looked**, and **behold**, a **great** multitude that no **one** could **number**, **from** every nation, from **all** **tribes** and **peoples** and **languages**, **standing** **before** the throne and before the **Lamb**, clothed in **white** **robes**, with palm **branches** in **their** **hands**, and **crying** **out** with a loud **voice**, "Salvation belongs to our **God** who **sits** on the throne, and to the Lamb!" And all the **angels** were standing around the throne and around the **elders** and the four **living** **creatures**, and they **fell** on their **faces** before the throne and worshiped God, **saying**, "Amen! **Blessing** and **glory** and **wisdom** and thanksgiving and honor and **power** and **might** be to our God forever and **ever**! Amen." Then one of the elders **addressed** me, saying, "Who are these, clothed in white robes, and from **where** have they **come**?" (ESV)

```
F E N U M B E R E W O P P Y
T R Y B Z M O L X Q C O M E
R E J R I E H T D E K O O L
I H L A N G U A G E S R D L
B W B N D L O H E B R V S E
E H G C E D C R O B E S I F
S I N H K V R R O U T J W A
L T I E Y G E E Y Q F D H F
E E V S O J A R S I A I A U
G N I D N A T S S S S N C N M
N O L M M S U E A I E G D I
A V B E F O R E Y S T D S G
L P E O P L E S I E F S T H
L A B L E S S I N G R E A T
F Q W Q Y R O L G V O I C E
H I Z S L Z D W L A M B K M
```

Solution on Page 353

We Honor the Lord

Romans 14:5–9

One person **decides** that one **day** is **holier** than **another**. Another person decides that **all** days are the **same**. **Every** person **must make** his **own** decision. When **people observe** a special day, they observe it to honor the **Lord**. When people **eat** all **kinds** of **foods**, they honor the Lord as they eat, **since** they **give thanks** to **God**. Vegetarians also honor the Lord when they eat, and they, too, give thanks to God. It's clear that we don't **live** to honor **ourselves**, and we don't **die** to honor ourselves. If we live, we honor the Lord, and if we die, we honor the Lord. So **whether** we live or die, we belong to the Lord. For this reason **Christ** died and **came back** to **life** so that he **would** be the Lord of **both** the living and the dead. (GW)

```
I A S H F R N B O E R W U I
C V H U L T B D Q T S U M C
V Y Y S Y I V K O T D K H P
O A H X A N F E A A N R P K
L D K H X B O E C N I S Z H
B R O C S F O O D S K S X P
Y O X M A A N O T H E R L J
O L T M O B S E R V E M L K
G X T H A N K S L O H V A D
X N Z E L P O E P O N Z I C
I Q M K W G S D L W L E A L
L A T A O R C I Y N V D V T
S H J M U C E C Z R X B K P
W L M O L R R E H T E H W A
Z H I T D B Y D O G I V E R
L K X G I U C G K O X B E C
```

Solution on Page 353

Prince of Peace

Isaiah 9:2–6

The **people** who walked in darkness have **seen** a **great** **light**; **those** who **dwelt** in a **land** of **deep** darkness, on them has light **shone**. You have multiplied the **nation**; you have increased its **joy**; they rejoice **before** you as with joy at the harvest, as they are **glad** when they **divide** the **spoil**. For the **yoke** of his **burden**, and the **staff** for his shoulder, the **rod** of his oppressor, you have broken as on the **day** of **Midian**. For **every** **boot** of the tramping warrior in **battle** tumult and every garment rolled in **blood** will be **burned** as **fuel** for the **fire**. For to us a **child** is **born**, to us a **son** is **given**; and the government **shall** be **upon** his shoulder, and his **name** shall be **called** Wonderful Counselor, **Mighty God**, Everlasting **Father**, Prince of **Peace**. (ESV)

```
E I X T O Z X K O C R H B F
M U N E E I O S R X D U P Q
A J P K D O O L B U R D E N
N E S O D E L L A C L S O O
B R D Y N R E H T A F T P S
R T O O B A D L T S H A L L
I J H B R Y E B L H U F E Z
O S E E N W E V E R Y F B E
Y A P R D H M L D F W I U V
T Z D Y N A I D I M O P R O
I H T A E R G T V O E R N X
F H Z C L I H O I E P A E G
D U A F V G T N D Z T S D O
C E E E I V Y D L I H C N D
P A N L G R T H O S E G A G
N Q S V J Y E N H N Y Y L U
```

Solution on Page 353

Smooth Talk

Proverbs 26:20–28

Without **wood** a **fire goes out**, and without **gossip** a quarrel **dies down**. As charcoal **fuels** burning **coals** and wood fuels fire, so a quarrelsome **person** fuels a dispute. The **words** of a gossip are swallowed greedily, and they go down **into** a person's innermost **being**. Like a **clay pot** covered with **cheap silver**, so is **smooth talk** that **covers** up an **evil** heart. Whoever is **filled** with **hate** disguises it with his **speech**, but **inside** he **holds** on to **deceit**. When he talks charmingly, do not **trust** him because of the **seven** disgusting **things** in his heart. His hatred is deceitfully **hidden**, but his wickedness will be revealed to the community. Whoever **digs** a **pit** will **fall** into it. Whoever rolls a **stone** will have it **roll back** on him. A **lying** tongue hates its victims, and a flattering mouth **causes ruin**. (GW)

```
D R J L G F R P I E T A L K
O G P D F U J F I R E I Q J
W Y O D I N S I D E V P S T
N O T N H S I L V E R I M H
W H R J S I D L Z I N T O I
H N Y D L O D E P E R S O N
W X E P S F L D C Y R U T G
R T J V U L J M E E D R H S
S P K E E Z A E V N I T O T
V B L P I S S O G Y E T L O
A S E S U A C P C C S H D N
E A G I G A L K E H L U S E
W F L E N S L V C E A A T W
S G A F I G O E S A C T Y V
D E U L Y I R U W P B H E G
Z Q T F L D J X T P R T A G
```

Solution on Page 354

Fed with Milk

1 Corinthians 3:1–7

And I, **brethren**, **could** not **speak** **unto** you as unto **spiritual**, but as unto carnal, as unto **babes** in **Christ**. I **fed** you with **milk**, not with meat; for ye were not yet **able** to **bear** it: **nay**, not **even** now are ye able; for ye are yet carnal: for **whereas** **there** is among you **jealousy** and strife, are ye not carnal, and do ye not **walk** **after** the **manner** of **men**? For when **one** **saith**, I am of **Paul**; and another, I am of **Apollos**; are ye not men? **What** then is Apollos? and what is Paul? **Ministers** **through** **whom** ye believed; and **each** as the **Lord** **gave** to him. I **planted**, Apollos **watered**; but **God** gave the **increase**. So then neither is he that planteth **anything**, neither he that watereth; but God that **giveth** the increase. (ASV)

```
Z J E A L O U S Y E U N T O
B S P E A K A P O L L O S H
T D P A U L N E O B V O I T
K L I M T A Y W D A S K R E
Z M V K I W T H R O U G H V
C H M A R N H O O V C O C I
S M S O I M I M L O G D N G
Z B A Y P P N S U E A C H V
H Z I N S Q G L T N R A E B
L G T N N I D W H E R E A S
G A H E A E E F A R R A W O
R V V M F Y R S B H F S T I
O E N O H R E D E T N A L P
X S P J T N T O E E R E H T
Q N W H Z I A R D R G J C T
H E I T A H W B A B E S X J
```

Solution on Page 354

Flesh and Blood

Hebrews 2:14–18

Since **all** of these sons and **daughters** have **flesh** and **blood**, **Jesus took** on flesh and blood to be like them. He **did** this so that by **dying** he **would destroy** the **one** who had **power over death** (that is, the devil). In this **way** he would **free those** who were **slaves** all **their lives** because they were **afraid** of dying. So Jesus helps Abraham's descendants rather than helping **angels**. Therefore, he had to **become** like his brothers and **sisters** so that he **could** be **merciful**. He **became** like them so that he could **serve** as a **faithful chief priest** in **God**'s **presence** and **make peace** with God for their **sins**. Because Jesus experienced temptation when he **suffered**, he is **able** to **help** others when they are **tempted**. (GW)

```
E L B A N P H F V O X A B Q
M E R C I F U L R D O O L B
O C E P M A K E A E D I D L
C A V S S I D U T S E I R P
E E O I T T G B A T A K Q W
B P N S A H K E V R E S V Z
V S R T T F Y C F O E W T H
D C C E Y U W A Y Y C W H E
V M R R S L D M K O O T O L
W S D S D E R E F F U S S P
B D L Y O E N O T T L H E X
X L F E I H C C Q P D T F F
G U I N G N Y C E O M A L V
P O U V F N G H S U S E J X
U W D S E V A L S Q S D T Z
N V U O L S R I E H T M Z Z
```

Solution on Page 354

Job Did Not Sin

Job 1:18–22

While he was **still** speaking, another messenger **arrived** with this **news**: "**Your** sons and daughters were feasting in **their oldest** brother's **home**. Suddenly, a powerful **wind swept** in **from** the wilderness and **hit** the **house** on **all** sides. The house collapsed, and all your children are **dead**. I am the only **one** who escaped to **tell** you." **Job stood** up and **tore** his **robe** in **grief**. Then he **shaved** his **head** and **fell** to the **ground** to worship. He **said**, "I **came naked** from my mother's **womb**, and I will be naked when I **leave**. The **LORD gave** me **what** I had, and the LORD has **taken** it **away**. **Praise** the **name** of the LORD!" In all of this, Job **did** not **sin** by blaming **God**. (NLT)

```
F E L L U U A B J W M A G S
Z Z P L Q O D N I W B V H Y
N I H I A I O D O G Y N C K
A B E T A I M M G Q H A Y D
M R D S D Q B O J R H A W F
E V A G U Q X D C Z B R R Z
C J S R P O S X T A Y O U R
D F E I R G H O H P M B H K
Y U R T A I A L E A V E R K
H K O R I K V D I D A D S S
D M S N S H E E R D H R T T
E G W W E A D S D N U O R G
U P E U F W E T F T O L M J
R P N R T A K E N D E A D E
T I H S O Y A Q W B O L R S
S X W H A T N C B Q C F L F
```

Solution on Page 354

I Received Mercy

1 Timothy 1:12–17

I **thank** him who has **given** me strength, **Christ Jesus** our **Lord**, **because** he **judged** me faithful, appointing me to his **service**, though formerly I was a blasphemer, persecutor, and **insolent opponent**. But I received **mercy** because I had **acted** ignorantly in unbelief, and the **grace** of our Lord overflowed for me with the **faith** and **love** that are in Christ Jesus. The **saying** is trustworthy and deserving of **full** acceptance, that Christ Jesus came **into** the **world** to **save sinners**, of **whom** I am the **foremost**. But I received mercy for this **reason**, that in me, as the foremost, Jesus Christ **might display** his **perfect patience** as an **example** to **those** who were to believe in him for **eternal life**. To the **King** of the **ages**, **immortal**, invisible, the **only God**, be **honor** and glory forever and **ever**. **Amen**. (ESV)

```
U E E V O L I N V G I G Z D
V Y V T T I B S E R V I C E
Z S H A C F B C M M C V X G
J E S U S E N Y F L A E S D
S G C L C E F O L O T N E U
I A K A I T R R O N O H L J
N F U T R E T N E N O P P O
N S A R M G T L J P Y R M L
E P C O T E O E V V H R A O
R T S M M S E D R T P D X R
S T S M N S A Y I N G K E D
O H D I S P L A Y Q A A V U
G A W G R I F C U O S L E X
V N Y H N H R T H O S E R Y
U K I T O E C E N F U L L H
K Z O K M M B D L R O W G K
```

Solution on Page 355

Have No Fear

The Gospel of Matthew 10:26–33

"So have no **fear** of them, for **nothing** is **covered** that will not be revealed, or hidden that will not be known. **What** I **tell** you in the **dark**, **say** in the **light**, and what you hear **whispered**, **proclaim** on the housetops. And do not fear **those** who **kill** the **body** but cannot kill the **soul**. **Rather** fear him who **can destroy both** soul and body in hell. Are not **two sparrows sold** for a penny? And not **one** of them will fall to the **ground apart from your** Father. But even the **hairs** of your **head** are **all** numbered. Fear not, therefore; you are of more value than **many** sparrows. So everyone who acknowledges me **before men**, I also will acknowledge before my Father who is in heaven, but whoever denies me before men, I also will **deny** before my Father who is in heaven." (ESV)

```
O T G S O U L J Z F A N O X
M A N Y O Y S C R H C K K O
V W I P Y L D Y B S Z W F I
T A H W T A D O V B O G N N
W V T I R E Q S B N Z R O O
X O O K S A Y P E G Q A W A
D Y N T Q P D A F R A E F M
E F R O M R E R O O Z M E O
N O E Y O O R R R R U E X R Z
Y A H W H C E O E N C N P F
O R T E L L V W U D K N A E
U B A F A A O S A C I L A C
R D F T H I C L R X L B D X
K G K F H M T H G I L O H A
S P X F T E S O H T A T E Y
Q P A X D T R A P A J H B K
```

Solution on Page 355

Don't Leave Me

Psalms 27:7–13

Hear me as I **pray**, O **LORD**. Be **merciful** and **answer** me! My heart has heard you **say**, "**Come** and **talk** with me." And my heart **responds**, "LORD, I am coming." Do not **turn your back** on me. Do not **reject** your servant in **anger**. You have **always** been my **helper**. Don't leave me now; don't abandon me, O **God** of my salvation! **Even** if my father and mother abandon me, the LORD will **hold** me close. **Teach** me how to **live**, O LORD. **Lead** me **along** the **right path**, for my **enemies** are **waiting** for me. Do not let me **fall into their hands**. For they accuse me of **things** I've never **done**; with every **breath** they **threaten** me with **violence**. Yet I am confident I will **see** the LORD's goodness **while** I am **here** in the **land** of the living. (NLT)

```
E S D N A H L L A F I D O G
A D E E T H U W D E D T Z D
T N M O H F M B B L N K F C
B O G N I T I A W I O R S Q
C P A C N W C X L H P H Y X
N S R N G K A N S W E R O P
E E Y A S H K E T R A A U A
M R T E C L C H E U L Y R T
A Q V A V N G Q H O R E S H
V E E S E I M E N E G N E K
I T D L R R L G P N D A E L
Q G O N M P H T A E R B G A
T I P V E N R T H E I R Q T
V L D R E J E C T D N A L T
B C D V A G I P P A L O R D
Q J E K A Y M V V C T H D D
```

Solution on Page 355

The Fringe of His Garment

The Gospel of Luke 8:43–48

And **there** was a **woman** who had had a **discharge** of **blood** for twelve **years**, and though she had **spent all** her **living** on **physicians**, she could not be healed by **anyone**. She **came** up **behind** him and touched the **fringe** of his **garment**, and immediately her discharge of blood **ceased**. And **Jesus** said, "Who was it that touched me?" When all **denied** it, **Peter** said, "Master, the **crowds** surround you and are **pressing** in on you!" But Jesus said, "Someone touched me, for I **perceive** that **power** has **gone out from** me." And when the woman **saw** that she was not **hidden**, she came **trembling**, and falling **down before** him **declared** in the **presence** of all the **people** why she had touched him, and how she had been immediately healed. And he said to her, "Daughter, your **faith** has **made** you **well**; go in peace." (ESV)

```
H L V Y D S O H F C D B N E
T G L E B O U R I E O Y W P
R N P A P D O S C D X U O S
H I E R E M D L E Y D W D O
E S X S F W A E B J E E G U
M S A T O R E G A R M E N T
A E T R E M B L I N G L I N
C R C D U Z F C L R X P V M
E P H Y S I C I A N S O I G
R R E W F B E H I N D E L H
E E A R U A C E G E N P T A
H S T C C S F I G O R I N Y
T E N E I E E N G C A Y K M
I N E D P G I B E F O R E D
I C P V Q R Y V I N A M O W
H E S P F M A D E N I E D Z
```

Solution on Page 355

Jesus Expels a Demon

The Gospel of Luke 4:31–36

And he **went** **down** to **Capernaum**, a **city** of Galilee. And he was **teaching** them on the **Sabbath**, and they were astonished at his teaching, for his **word** **possessed** **authority**. And in the **synagogue** there was a **man** who had the **spirit** of an **unclean** demon, and he **cried** **out** with a loud **voice**, "Ha! **What** have you to do with us, **Jesus** of **Nazareth**? Have you **come** to **destroy** us? I **know** who you are—the **Holy** **One** of God." But Jesus **rebuked** him, **saying**, "Be **silent** and come out of him!" And when the demon had **thrown** him down in **their** **midst**, he **came** out of him, **having** done him no **harm**. And they were **all** amazed and **said** to one another, "What is this word? For with authority and **power** he commands the unclean spirits, and they come out!" (ESV)

```
D M L E P C Y R R I E H T C
N R M L O T T D E S T R O Y
V A O M N H I E W B O A G X
C H E W G R R S O D U N H J
C R D L B O O S P J I K E W
P H L U C W H E T Y X R E B
K A T H J N T S A N T B T D
F Y I A I C U S K W E Y I O
I D D V B M A O T E A L R W
K S I I A B G P A N C O I N
G T A N A Z A R E T H H P S
Q C S G D J W S S R I U S T
I Y M D E U G O G A N Y S Y
E L T S I J D M N I G A K O
X T U I R M X L E K S S U P
P S W E C I O V N L T T E M
```

Solution on Page 356

The Lamb Breaks the Seventh Seal

Revelation 8:1–5

When the **Lamb** **broke** the seventh **seal** on the **scroll**, **there** was **silence** throughout **heaven** for about **half** an hour. I **saw** the **seven** angels who **stand** **before** **God**, and they were **given** seven trumpets. Then another **angel** with a gold **incense** **burner** **came** and **stood** at the **altar**. And a **great** amount of incense was given to him to **mix** with the **prayers** of God's **people** as an **offering** on the gold altar before the throne. The **smoke** of the incense, mixed with the prayers of God's **holy** people, **ascended** up to God **from** the altar **where** the angel had poured them **out**. Then the angel **filled** the incense burner with **fire** from the altar and **threw** it **down** **upon** the **earth**; and **thunder** **crashed**, lightning **flashed**, and there was a terrible earthquake. (NLT)

```
H D B W E E Y P B E R E H W
R Y O R A T L A H U B H J E
W U E O R S O P P R E U F R
S D N A T S H S O K D J E H
F C V W H S R K O E O O U T
G J R R O E E M H U P O N H
O S D O Y D S S E A L Q E E
N C N A L N A N E D U S B R
E E R F O L G R E A T D R E
V P V L F W O H B C I E C D
E D A A F F S D X L N N A N
S M G H E A W M E R E I M U
B G I B R H E X U L F G E H
M O V C I B U B I B L R N T
A D E D N E C S A M I I O A
Q W N G G P C V O F J Z F M
```

Solution on Page 356

The Man Born Blind

The Gospel of John 9:1–7

As **Jesus** was **walking** along, he **saw** a **man** who had been **blind** **from** **birth**. "Rabbi," his **disciples** **asked** him, "why was this man **born** blind? Was it because of his **own** **sins** or his parents' sins?" "It was not because of his sins or his parents' sins," Jesus **answered**. "This **happened** so the power of **God** could be **seen** in him. We must **quickly** carry **out** the tasks **assigned** us by the **one** who **sent** us. The **night** is **coming**, and then no one **can** **work**. But **while** I am **here** in the world, I am the **light** of the world." Then he **spit** on the ground, made **mud** with the saliva, and **spread** the mud **over** the blind man's **eyes**. He **told** him, "Go **wash** yourself in the **pool** of Siloam" (Siloam **means** "sent"). So the man **went** and washed and came **back** seeing! (NLT)

```
P D N T M T C P C C W X H C
C L C F A L M C L S H S A W
Z O C A N E E S T X A N H F
M T M G B K D N W E B I M C
L O D I T H J A R C L U N B
I C R A N S W E R E D O W Q
G T N F P G H M T I E A O R
H U H I Q G I J S H N Z B P
T O T A O U N C J S G J O U
M I W B P O I I T E I I R A
I Q D S L P N C K X S N N W
T N E W L I E R K L S U S B
R Y K E K B N N W L A R S X
E G S P R E A D E A Y W E M
V N A Z O E O C D D A F N V
O K O A W G B E K S O V T A
```

Solution on Page 356

Joyful Song

Psalms 33:1–9

Joyfully **sing** to the **LORD**, you righteous **people**. Praising the LORD is **proper** for **decent** people. **Give thanks** with a **lyre** to the LORD. **Make music** for him on a ten-stringed **harp**. Sing a **new song** to him. **Play** beautifully and joyfully on stringed instruments. The word of the LORD is **correct**, and everything he does is trustworthy. The LORD **loves** righteousness and justice. His **mercy fills** the earth. The **heavens** were **made** by the word of the LORD and **all** the stars by the **breath** of his **mouth**. He gathers the **water** in the **sea** like a **dam** and **puts** the **oceans** in his storehouses. Let all the earth **fear** the LORD. Let all who **live** in the **world stand** in **awe** of him. He **spoke**, and it **came into being**. He **gave** the order, and **there** it **stood**. (GW)

```
K N X T J G C H Z M P A R J
V F R P Z F E H U Y X O T T
I Q G S I L X S M O U T H S
V I G I A F I K Q E O N E S
U Z K N V C D N K A R I R L
M I N G O E V A G L H C E R
G Q C A G S M H P L O U Y M
E W A X U S Z T T R R R A S
W J M S T O O D R A A D D O
O C E A N S N E V A E H L H
R A N E W L C C P O F R H N
L D R E I T J E G N I E B Z
D Y P R T C O N E K O P S T
L I A Y V P F T S E V O L U
N K S L L I F W A T E R A E
L I V E P H I Y S T U P X K
```

Solution on Page 356

Jacob Wrestles

Genesis 32:22–28

During that **night** he got up and **gathered** his **two** wives, his two **slaves** and his **eleven** children and crossed at the **shallow part** of the **Jabbok** River. After he **sent** them **across** the **stream**, he sent everything **else** across. So **Jacob** was **left alone**. Then a **man wrestled** with him **until** dawn. When the man **saw** that he **could** not **win against** Jacob, he **touched** the **socket** of Jacob's **hip** so that it was **dislocated** as they wrestled. Then the man said, "Let me go; it's **almost** dawn." But Jacob **answered**, "I won't let you go until you **bless** me." So the man **asked** him, "What's **your name**?" "Jacob," he answered. The man said, "Your name will no **longer** be Jacob but **Israel** [He Struggles With God], **because** you have **struggled** with **God** and with men—and you have won." (GW)

```
G N A W O I U J P Z T Q J W
R D E L G G U R T S A W S X
S E I V O B Z E A L M O S T
A R Y S E N S D G A P E M L
W E N O L L E L A N I G H T
I H N B E O E E I S H L N S
N T R A P A C M N W V E L W
Q A W S R B P A S E S A X S
P G M S B L D N T R V A F O
W J I O D E L T S E R W R J
M A D R H S C C S D D U Z J
A B L C O S H A L L O W T A
E B U A L I T N U Y T M S C
R O O I T E K C O S F K T O
T K C O O R L O N G E R M B
S A E M S T Y G O D L E A Y
```

Solution on Page 357

He Chose Us

Ephesians 1:3–9

Praise the **God** and **Father** of our **Lord Jesus Christ**! Through Christ, God has blessed us with **every spiritual** blessing that **heaven** has to **offer**. **Before** the **creation** of the **world**, he chose us through Christ to be **holy** and **perfect** in his presence. Because of his **love** he had **already decided** to **adopt** us through Jesus Christ. He freely chose to do this so that the kindness he had **given** us in his **dear Son** would be praised and given glory. Through the **blood** of his Son, we are **set free from** our **sins**. God forgives our **failures** because of his overflowing kindness. He poured **out** his kindness by giving us every **kind** of **wisdom** and **insight** when he revealed the **mystery** of his **plan** to us. He had decided to do this through Christ. (GW)

```
V S W X R G I E F A Q E V K
B O U T T V M N D F S N Z X
Y T V S B M C X P L Z C F F
U K D P E V W H U J O L L R
T E T L F J G G R B Z O Y O
H H E V O L I D N I K F R M
A S G P R V N O S V S N E O
T M I I E Y L O H P A T V D
T Y K N S R F A I L U R E S
C S B X S N F R P T Y D F I
Q T L W H L I E Q M A R K W
Y E O J O T D E C I D E D K
L R O R U R G U R T I H R Q
H Y D A E R L A D O P T R C
O R L F R E E D N E V A E H
V V K G O D B U R E F F O S
```

Solution on Page 357

Jesus Is Lord of the Sabbath

The Gospel of Mark 2:23–28

And it **came** to **pass**, that he was going on the sabbath **day** **through** the **grainfields**; and his disciples **began**, as they **went**, to **pluck** the **ears**. And the **Pharisees** **said** **unto** him, **Behold**, why do they on the sabbath day that **which** is not **lawful**? And he said unto them, **Did** ye never read what David did, when he had **need**, and was **hungry**, he, and they that were with him? How he **entered** **into** the **house** of **God** when Abiathar was **high** **priest**, and **ate** the showbread, which it is not lawful to eat **save** for the priests, and **gave** also to them that were with him? And he said unto them, The sabbath was made for **man**, and not man for the sabbath: so that the **Son** of man is **lord** **even** of the sabbath. (ASV)

```
Q F F G C U Y E A D J U T X
B C J Z Q D N F V P I E Y B
K W T J C U Q T L A H V Z D
H M S D H G I H O U S E X J
S R D E T B I K N T F N E D
G S L E E H W G X P N W T R
W C E N T E R E D F B I A O
I C I E N Y Y O B D N C W L
C K F T S N A M U O B C Q V
H N O P R I E S T G E P W F
A N U N A A R M N W H I C H
I D S O E R K A A P O C K V
C O A S J G G U H C L H R H
N K I Y A E R C W P D U I F
X I D V B P T H K W O I C N
W B E V K M W G W E Y K D K
```

Solution on Page 357

The Sixth Seal

Revelation 6:12–16

I **watched** as the **Lamb** **broke** the **sixth** seal, and there was a great earthquake. The **sun** **became** as **dark** as **black** **cloth**, and the moon became as **red** as **blood**. Then the **stars** of the **sky** **fell** to the **earth** like green **figs** falling **from** a tree **shaken** by a strong **wind**. The sky was **rolled** up like a scroll, and **all** of the **mountains** and islands were **moved** from **their** **places**. Then everyone—the **kings** of the earth, the **rulers**, the generals, the wealthy, the **powerful**, and **every** **slave** and free person—all **hid** themselves in the **caves** and among the **rocks** of the mountains. And they **cried** to the mountains and the rocks, "Fall on us and hide us from the **face** of the **one** who **sits** on the throne and from the **wrath** of the Lamb." (NLT)

```
T K C A L B E C A M E C A F
V T A O Y I N O O K A N Y U
Y P O W E R F U L I R I U E
Q R I R S L N Y K S T A R S
O D E H C T A W Y Q H P D V
I M X V A D L M M T S H W M
V J C I E E O L B R T I C O
S N N Q T L M O E O I D N R
W S E C A L P L L F S E I F
O I R K C O U C K B S Q I T
S A N V A R E I D R J G U D
J L Z D V H N C E O S J G T
E L A E E G S D O K I E Q X
Z J B V S I F S C E X P M F
N J C O E D R O P H T A R W
D E P M J J R C X T H E I R
```

Solution on Page 357

Always Seek His Presence

Psalms 105:1–10

Give **thanks** to the **LORD**. Call on him. **Make** **known** **among** the **nations** **what** he has **done**. **Sing** to him. Make **music** to **praise** him. Meditate on **all** the **miracles** he has performed. **Brag** **about** his **holy** **name**. Let the hearts of **those** who **seek** the LORD **rejoice**. Search for the LORD and his **strength**. Always seek his **presence**. **Remember** the miracles he performed, the **amazing** **things** he **did**, and the judgments he pronounced, you descendants of his **servant** Abraham, you descendants of **Jacob**, his **chosen** ones. He is the LORD our **God**. His judgments are pronounced throughout the **earth**. He always remembers his **promise**, the **word** that he **commanded** for a thousand generations, the promise that he **made** to Abraham, and his sworn **oath** to **Isaac**. He confirmed it as a **law** for Jacob, as an everlasting promise to **Israel**. (GW)

```
D H A U I H D E Q P J M K T
S C J H D T C S G Z M V N H
N K M O H G N I Z A M A O Z
C L N I M N V A L L V L W L
A E N A M E R R D R Y M N G
A G D G H R N P E I U M N G
S E I W D T E S K S D I A L
I N O A R S S B I R S R M U
M A A B O U T C M A B A E B
Z R N T L P R E S E N C E E
G W E X I R B V G L M L P G
O A S J C O M M A N D E D A
D R O W O M N W K O O S R P
Q U H J Q I J S E K A M D Y
B O C A J S C G E H T R A E
G T H O S E Q E S W H A T X
```

Solution on Page 358

The Hands of Compassionate Women

Lamentations 4:6–10

For the chastisement of the daughter of my **people** has been **greater** than the punishment of **Sodom**, **which** was overthrown in a **moment**, and no **hands** were **wrung** for her. Her **princes** were **purer** than snow, whiter than **milk**; **their bodies** were more **ruddy** than **coral**, the **beauty** of their **form** was like sapphire. Now their **face** is blacker than **soot**; they are not recognized in the **streets**; their **skin** has shriveled on their **bones**; it has **become** as **dry** as **wood**. **Happier** were the **victims** of the **sword** than the victims of **hunger**, who **wasted away**, **pierced** by **lack** of the **fruits** of the **field**. The hands of compassionate **women** have **boiled** their **own** children; they **became** their **food during** the destruction of the daughter of my people. (ESV)

```
S R E R U P D E W C A I F V
M I L K F O Y K C A L S M G
C T P O O A S D N A H W M W
C S O W A S T E D V F O S Y
K D E O T O V E N U D R R J
U L P I S J S O M O R D S Y
G S U Q D M C N S O B T N A
H R O F I O R Y R N C N W W
F P O T R S B E C A M E O A
P R C A N S T B I N C M B J
M I L D S A T E G P E O H T
V N E U E H F A E N P M C F
H C Q R E X I U U R U A I T
T E G I C K E T U E T R H W
E S R N V E L Y N I K S W L
H U N G E R D E L I O B Q J
```

Solution on Page 358

In the Beginning

Genesis 1:1–7

In the **beginning God created** the **heaven** and the **earth**. And the earth was **without form**, and **void**; and darkness was **upon** the **face** of the **deep**. And the **Spirit** of God **moved** upon the face of the **waters**. And God said, "Let **there** be **light**": and there was light. And God **saw** the light, that it was good: and God divided the light **from** the darkness. And God **called** the light **Day**, and the darkness he called **Night**. And the **evening** and the **morning** were the **first** day. And God said, "Let there be a firmament in the **midst** of the waters, and let it **divide** the waters from the waters." And God **made** the firmament, and divided the waters **which** were **under** the firmament from the waters which were **above** the firmament. (KJV)

```
M R E E U G M B M Z J Y A S
H A Z D G U N D E R O T O I
P G N I N N I G E B N X X U
E T U O H T I W N T H C P L
C M O V E D L N T I A O Z A
A Y S C A E E E R L N E S J
W K A T V R T E L O I E R G
V F Y O E W R E P Y M G V C
A U B M N E D L A P A F H E
E A R T H F I H H T D R U T
K O X T B I V Q W C E O X H
F N S P I R I T S D I M F G
H T J A R S D F A O A H A I
M B F W A T E R S G K Y W N
K Z C L V K Z V Q X Z Z A L
L B S X D B F V R U N C S R
```

Solution on Page 358

Taxes to Caesar

The Gospel of Mark 12:13–17

And they send **unto** him **certain** of the Pharisees and of the **Herodians**, that they **might catch** him in **talk**. And when they were come, they **say** unto him, "**Teacher**, we **know** that **thou art true**, and carest not for any **one**; for thou regardest not the person of **men**, but of a truth teachest the **way** of **God**: Is it **lawful** to **give** tribute unto Caesar, or not? **Shall** we give, or shall we not give?" But he, knowing **their hypocrisy**, said unto them, "Why make ye **trial** of me? **Bring** me a denarius, that I **may see** it." And they **brought** it. And he saith unto them, "Whose is this image and superscription?" And they said unto him, "Caesar's." And **Jesus** said unto them, "**Render** unto Caesar the **things** that are Caesar's, and unto God the things that are God's." And they marveled **greatly** at him. (ASV)

```
B Y X E R T M P T Z M I E C
O L P P J C T L R D D D Q Q Y
J T E A C H E R P M C L F B
H A N K O M I G H T T V Y L
F E L U W R I E H T M L M V
E R R E D O G I Y R L B Z W
P G S O T J N L P I A Q G G
D Z A U D G N K O A G S I N
N R Y T S I C B C L E Y V I
H T A G A E A P R E D N E R
D R W T I L J N I O L V W B
R U R H O K K C S F U J A M
I E S A N E M A Y A F G A H
C Z L Q E H L Y P R W Q H B
O L L O E F T H C T A C X T
R D X W Z M S H A L L F C H
```

Solution on Page 358

Faith the Size of a Mustard Seed

The Gospel of Matthew 17:14–20

When they came to a crowd, a **man** came up to **Jesus**, **knelt** in front of him, and said, "Sir, have **mercy** on my **son**. He **suffers from seizures**. **Often** he **falls into fire** or **water**. I brought him to your **disciples**, but they couldn't **cure** him." Jesus **replied**, "You unbelieving and **corrupt generation**! How **long must** I be with you? How long must I put up with you? **Bring** him **here** to me!" Jesus **ordered** the **demon** to **come out** of the **boy**. At that **moment** the boy was cured. Then the disciples came to Jesus **privately** and **asked**, "Why couldn't we **force** the demon out of the boy?" He **told** them, "Because you have so **little faith**. I **can guarantee** this **truth**: If your faith is the **size** of a mustard **seed**, you can **say** to this mountain, 'Move from here to there,' and it will move. Nothing will be impossible for you." (GW)

```
M T O X P V H X X N J B O H
P U E Z I S U F F E R S U E
N Y S Y J B I G W I E Z T R
O U S T L E N K N I C U R E
I M O R F M S G Z O D I U D
T M N P A P C U F G L T T C
A I D N L T R O S U Y L H C
R Y R I L E R I R A C T F R
E E A N S C P R V R I O L H
N O P N E C D S F A U I M M
E B D L O T I E F N T P K E
G I W N I N F P R T D E T R
A T A O O E S O L E R F L C
G C T M R M D E K E D I D Y
P N E W Y O B S E Q S R A A
I D R S T M A G W D T E O S
```

Solution on Page 359

Consider the Lilies

The Gospel of Luke 12:22–27

Therefore I **tell** you, do not be **anxious** **about** **your** **life**, **what** you will **eat**, **nor** about your **body**, what you will put on. For life is more than **food**, and the body more than clothing. Consider the **ravens**: they neither **sow** nor reap, they have neither storehouse nor **barn**, and yet **God** **feeds** them. Of how **much** more value are you than the **birds**! And **which** of you by **being** anxious **can** **add** a **single** **hour** to his **span** of life? If then you are not **able** to do as small a **thing** as that, why are you anxious about the **rest**? Consider the **lilies**, how they **grow**: they neither **toil** nor **spin**, yet I tell you, **even** Solomon in **all** his **glory** was not **arrayed** like **one** of **these**. (ESV)

```
U R A N X I O U S M C Q R M
K J D R S H N L L U N D P V
A A K W R H C I H W X N W M
A B H D Q A O L P L E V S S
C A L T O T Y I V L U V T P
T F E E D S N E V A R I E A
E H B L C R L S D H B A R N
T N I L A G W C O E M O M R
A S R N N L O U I F Z D U K
R O D I G O R N O I I O C T
I Q S O T R G F X L Y G H K
L L C H I Y D O B O N E A T
D I M Y U L A O I R S M T M
Q P U C O Q F D S E O P G L
E L D X C Q B A D S W V I U
P H S X Q B V E Y T L R O N
```

Solution on Page 359

God Is a Rock

Psalms 18:31–38

For who is **God**, but the **LORD**? And who is a **rock**, **except** our God?—the God who **equipped** me with strength and **made** my way blameless. He made my **feet** like the feet of a **deer** and **set** me secure on the **heights**. He **trains** my hands for **war**, so that my **arms** **can** **bend** a **bow** of **bronze**. You have **given** me the **shield** of **your** salvation, and your **right** **hand** supported me, and your gentleness made me **great**. You **gave** a **wide** **place** for my **steps** **under** me, and my feet **did** not **slip**. I **pursued** my **enemies** and overtook them, and did not **turn** **back** **till** they were **consumed**. I **thrust** them **through**, so that they were not **able** to rise; they **fell** under my feet. (ESV)

Solution on Page 359

```
A W A K C A B A E N S I S E
H X C X U R E I D D N L Y D
E O C B D M C N G L I R F R
R U O Y G S A P I P A D A O
A W D U V H L A V U R S B L
W G E Q U I P P E D T T L B
Y L M L E E H C N H D E E P
Q S U F D L T G G E F Z T S
D P S E A D W I U W N O H C
M E N E M I E S L O G E R D
N T O T D H R V R L R T U Y
S S C E R U J B A E E H S S
E Z U T P E C X E G A G T O
S I K D Y U D D O G T I U T
P C L C W B E N D V H R R E
H D W N I M L X U M C A N I
```

Solution on Page 359

A House on Solid Rock

The Gospel of Matthew 7:22–27

"On **judgment** **day** **many** will **say** to me, '**Lord**! Lord! We prophesied in your **name** and **cast** **out** **demons** in your name and **performed** many **miracles** in your name.' But I will **reply**, 'I **never** **knew** you. Get **away** **from** me, you who **break** God's laws.' **Anyone** who **listens** to my **teaching** and **follows** it is **wise**, like a **person** who builds a house on **solid** **rock**. Though the **rain** comes in **torrents** and the floodwaters **rise** and the **winds** **beat** **against** that house, it won't **collapse** **because** it is **built** on bedrock. But anyone who **hears** my teaching and doesn't **obey** it is **foolish**, like a person who builds a house on sand. When the rains and **floods** **come** and the winds beat against that house, it will collapse with a **mighty** crash." (NLT)

```
M S P W O U Y R L T R Y C C
B R E A K U T C G O B F A A
D N R D D S T N E R R O T S
K C F R H S I L O O F L O T
A S O I A H X A B U I L T Y
A L R L C I W G J G I O M V
N S M A L A N A U D Y W O C
B N E V Y A J I D X A S O Y
  I T D L G B P N G R D M N F
E S U A C E B S M R E A B D
W I N D S A H T E N M V R P
S R A E H T R A N Y O N E P
G O S R T U E I T F N R P N
F L O O D S S N M R S W L A
I C Y T H G I M S O B E Y M
K A S S Y J R L N M W I S E
```

Solution on Page 359

The Day of the Lord

Obadiah 1:15–18

"The **day** of the LORD is **near** for **all** nations. Edom, you will be **treated** as you have treated others. You will get **back** **what** you have **given**. As you, **Israel**, **drank** on my **holy** mountain, so all nations will **drink** in **turn**. They will drink and **guzzle** **down** **everything** in it. They will be like **those** who have **never** **existed**. But **refugees** will **live** on **Mount** Zion. It will be holy. The descendants of **Jacob** will get back **their** possessions. The descendants of Jacob will be like a **fire**. The descendants of **Joseph** will be like a **flame**. But the descendants of **Esau** will be like **straw**. They will be **burned** and destroyed. There will be no **one** **left** among the descendants of Esau." The LORD has **spoken**. (GW)

```
D R W G W T S N K W X K H V
Q E N A N H G Z B O H D X Z
L Z T L R I A U T D J U L C
C E A H A T H T Z H U R S P
N N E K O P S T U Z R U N W
N E R N E S A U Y R L E F T
B Q B S E D E B U R N E D F
S D O W N R E F U G E E S X
Q J C E R I F R R N I V D K
T Y A J Q N D E T S I X E O
V R J W E K M V H O L Y T M
X K L V Z A O E E M K C A B
E V I L L D U N I S R A E L
M G S F A E N O R K N A R D
U Z H Y P Z T V J E F K T U
O G T P F A H Z A F Q A A D
```

Solution on Page 360

A Fresh Olive Leaf

Genesis 8:6–12

After **another** forty **days**, **Noah opened** the **window** he had **made** in the **boat** and released a **raven**. The **bird flew back** and **forth until** the floodwaters on the **earth** had dried up. He **also** released a **dove** to **see** if the **water** had receded and it could **find dry** ground. But the dove could find no **place** to **land** because the water **still** covered the ground. So it returned to the boat, and Noah **held out** his **hand** and drew the dove back **inside**. After waiting another seven days, Noah released the dove **again**. This **time** the dove returned to him in the evening with a **fresh olive leaf** in its **beak**. Then Noah **knew** that the floodwaters were **almost gone**. He **waited** another seven days and then released the dove again. This time it **did** not **come** back. (NLT)

```
F B N W W D E U M I T B T L
A N O T H E R E T F A L S O
P L E X S D N Y V C O D I D
X Y M W I N O K K K B C N W
V Y I O N I A G A M W A C N
I G T D S F H E S D L E H D
J P C N I T B V D D M F L L
H T P I D E N E P O R D X F
Q A S W E T T S C E U I W P
H F Q Y C I G U S W B Y B L
G Y U E A R T H T R O F D L
P J N W L D U I E L A N O O
H M T L P Y O T I E A V V G
P O I I M U A V L H M L E O
N T L O U W E J E M E X W N
S I O H J U I K K Y M A D E
```

Solution on Page 360

The Scroll

Revelation 5:1–5

I **saw** a **scroll** in the **right hand** of the **one** who **sits** on the throne. It had **writing both** on the **inside** and on the outside. It was sealed with **seven seals**. I saw a **powerful angel** calling **out** in a loud **voice**, "Who deserves to **open** the scroll and **break** the seals on it?" No one in **heaven**, on **earth**, or **under** the earth could open the scroll or **look** inside it. I **cried bitterly** because no one was found who **deserved** to open the scroll or look inside it. Then one of the **leaders** said to me, "Stop **crying**! The Lion **from** the **tribe** of **Judah**, the **Root** of **David**, has won the **victory**. He **can** open the scroll and the seven seals on it." (GW)

Solution on Page 350

```
W D G V I C T O R Y X H M D
W A S R E D A E L W K M M S
U Q T D E S E R V E D O M O
E U L U F R E W O P Q J O C
Y G M E O T Q S J U O U R L
S N N G T I G U E L H I F L
A L E I C A N E V A E H N L
Z M B V T D I S N D L G D O
O S Q M E I Y D I K B S N H
G E U R F S R E C D R E P A
Y T P U K N C W H D E N G D
E F Z T C E A R T H A T V U
I Y F I O P N I O D K V O J
O I G I M O Q G B L S T I S
R I Y D S P R H H A L R C D
N G E L V M C T R I B E E H
```

Solution on Page 360

Heirs with Christ

Romans 8:12–17

So then, **brothers**, we are **debtors**, not to the flesh, to **live** according to the flesh. For if you live according to the flesh you will die, but if by the **Spirit** you put to **death** the **deeds** of the **body**, you will live. For **all** who are **led** by the Spirit of **God** are **sons** of God. For you **did** not **receive** the spirit of **slavery** to fall **back into fear**, but you have received the Spirit of **adoption** as sons, by **whom** we **cry**, "Abba! Father!" The Spirit **himself** **bears witness** with our spirit that we are **children** of God, and if children, then **heirs**—heirs of God and **fellow** heirs with **Christ**, **provided** we **suffer** with him in **order** that we **may** also be **glorified** with him. (ESV)

```
X J V A A M A O C A W C Z S
A Y D C B D M P S A I H O N
V X Z O E G O D R W L I S O
M A N O A H H P O O O L R S
G O Y Q R T W L T V I D B P
L Z T M S A L N B I E R W K
O W T K U E I Z E R O E V S
R B S L F D Z F D T I N X W
I E I S F T D L H S R O E V
F A R P E O H E I R S Z V D
I M H I R N R S D H P S I E
E N C R C S T M U I R D E L
D A Z I F D N I M K V D C U
K T Y T W E P H W C Y O E C
M J L I V E A S L A V E R Y
X M O B O D Y R M B A Y U P
```

Solution on Page 360

God Blessed the Seventh Day

Genesis 2:2–6

And on the **seventh day God finished** his **work which** he had made; and he **rested** on the seventh day **from all** his work which he had made. And God **blessed** the seventh day, and hallowed it; because that in it he rested from all his work which God had **created** and made. **These** are the generations of the heavens and of the **earth** when they were created, in the day that **Jehovah** God made earth and **heaven**. And no **plant** of the **field** was yet in the earth, and no **herb** of the field had yet **sprung** up; for Jehovah God had not **caused** it to **rain upon** the earth: and there was not a **man** to **till** the **ground**; but there **went** up a **mist** from the earth, and **watered** the **whole face** of the ground. (ASV)

```
S K C G H U F O H B S W T Y
X Z R R V A W O M Q E I H C
G C J O E L D A A N I T A S
N O P U W A N B T J N U Z S
N M G N Y B T E R E S E H T
T M K D O G L E V E R A I N
B F I N I S H E D A H E P T
F E L S T U S E S T E F D N
Y W O G T I T L P S J H L Q
N Q H V Y S Z L K B E Z E J
C Q T Z E J A A S C H D I E
Z S P R U N G D A M O R F L
Q V F W T F V F S P V H X O
J R O I W V T U I E A R T H
D D L Q F M O H C I H W W W
N L O D I T T U R G R H F B
```

Solution on Page 361

A Good Soldier of Christ Jesus

2 Timothy 2:1–8

My **child**, **find** **your** **source** of strength in the kindness of **Christ** **Jesus**. You've **heard** my **message**, and it's been confirmed by **many** witnesses. **Entrust** this message to faithful individuals who will be competent to **teach** others. **Join** me in suffering like a **good** soldier of Christ Jesus. Whoever **serves** in the military doesn't get **mixed** up in non-military activities. This pleases his commanding **officer**. Whoever **enters** an athletic competition **wins** the **prize** **only** when playing by the **rules**. A hard-working **farmer** **should** have the **first** **share** of the **crops**. Understand **what** I'm **saying**. The **Lord** will **help** you understand **all** **these** things. Always **think** **about** Jesus Christ. He was **brought** **back** to **life** and is a descendant of **David**. This is the Good **News** that I **tell** others. (GW)

```
J Y O C K T D N A I I S V R
Q M D Y Q P I T T H E S E M M
I D L U O H S E R V E S M I
Y N I S J I H L A W R A L X
O U H V O C D L K E N E R E
U P C W A U L N T Y Z N S D
R N G E E D R N I T H I N K
Z W T R R R E C I F F O R Z
Z T I T A W N U E S I J Y P
U P I N H E T N S F U R W O
F V A R S G R T E S I S S Z
Z N T E A A U Y L W P L E T
O M A M Y S S O U O S L G J
V C H R I S T N R Z A O E C
O H W A N E K C A B O U T H
O A H F G M L O R D K P Y A
```

Solution on Page 361

God Tells Noah of the Flood

Genesis 6:13–17

God **said** to **Noah**, "I have decided to put an **end** to **all** **people** **because** the **earth** is **full** of **their** violence. Now I'm going to **destroy** them along with the earth. **Make** yourself a **ship** of **cypress** **wood**. Make rooms in the ship and **coat** it inside and **out** with **tar**. This is how you should **build** it: the ship is to be 450 **feet** **long**, 75 feet **wide**, and 45 feet **high**. Make a **roof** for the ship, and **leave** an 18-inch-high opening at the **top**. Put a **door** in the **side** of the ship. Build the ship with **lower**, **middle**, and **upper** **decks**. I'm about to send a **flood** on the earth to destroy all people **under** the sky—every **living**, **breathing** **human**. **Everything** on earth will die." (GW)

Solution on Page 351

```
E W E V E R Y T H I N G G K
U D C Y D C M U W E N N D N
L O S R I E A O L I O I L J
O O A H S U K A V L C H I Y
W W W T I P E I X D U T U J
A I P E O P L E S M D A B Q
U N D E R E D D A U E E O X
N Z D E A R D N Y Z C R P G
T M P V L X I E A A K B F E
R Q E A L L M D U D S S K V
F T A R U M S S E R P Y C S
A O R O F X E S S A I P N F
R P J O L S T A O C R E Y E
G Z S F O R I J P C U T H E
U M V G O D N O A H G I H T
O Q Z Y D U D E X S S B N M
```

Solution on Page 361

Teach Us to Number Our Days

Psalms 90:11–17

Who knoweth the **power** of thine **anger**, and **thy** wrath **according** to the **fear** that is **due unto** thee? So **teach** us to **number** our **days**, that we **may** get us a **heart** of **wisdom**. Return, O **Jehovah**; how **long**? And let it **repent** thee **concerning** thy **servants**. Oh **satisfy** us in the **morning** with thy loving kindness, that we may **rejoice** and be **glad all** our days. Make us glad according to the days **wherein** thou **hast afflicted** us, and the years wherein we have **seen evil**. Let thy **work appear** unto thy servants, and thy glory **upon** their **children**. And let the **favor** of the **Lord** our **God** be upon us; and **establish** thou the work of our **hands** upon us; **yea**, the work of our hands establish thou it. (ASV)

```
L G L D E T S R T M H U M A
X Y A M O D S I W E M K F G
G B Y E A P P E A R A R R Y
J F E A R T U R R F F O E F
R G A E G D T T F V V W P S
D N W C L N H L R A A G E I
X O A I E P I A F E L N N T
P L V O S C A D V O G I T A
L E G J T G W C R O Y N L S
G R O E A N H D A O H R A E
W L D R B I E H M S C E B E
U H A T L N R S Y A D C J N
V C S D I R E B M U N N A F
C A R Y S O I V P N R O A G
H E R S H M N O O T M C X H
N T W B L T N M A O E R A B
```

Solution on Page 361

Truly God Has Listened

Psalms 66:13–20

I will **come** **into** **your** **house** with **burnt** offerings; I will **perform** my **vows** to you, that **which** my **lips** **uttered** and my **mouth** promised when I was in **trouble**. I will **offer** to you burnt offerings of fattened animals, with the **smoke** of the sacrifice of **rams**; I will **make** an offering of **bulls** and goats. **Selah.** Come and **hear**, **all** you who **fear** **God**, and I will **tell** **what** he has **done** for my **soul**. I **cried** to him with my mouth, and **high** **praise** was on my **tongue**. If I had cherished iniquity in my heart, the **Lord** **would** not have listened. But **truly** God has listened; he has attended to the **voice** of my **prayer**. **Blessed** be God, **because** he has not rejected my prayer or **removed** his steadfast **love** **from** me! (ESV)

```
Q X L Q M T E L L U P M U R
F X S I H N S K E O S A R D
P E M E P X E Z T W V K C I
J D A M M S M N O N M E E M
V R R R U R I V O K H K W A
A R U O Y W O U L D J Q C H
O W H F T I K Y E L E O L G
R V S R C D X R L F M I O I
W B L E S S E D B E P V R H
B E L P L T D V U K R E D C
X C A Y T A H W O O A S K I
P A K U L O H T R M Y I K H
B U L L S U N F T S E A Q W
U S O U L R R G O D R R E G
C E C G U O H T U O M P Y X
N N W B M Z H E R E F F O H
```

Solution on Page 362

You Sent Abundant Rain

Psalms 68:7–14

O **God**, when you **led** your people **out from Egypt**, when you **marched** through the **dry** wasteland, Interlude the **earth** trembled, and the **heavens** poured **down rain before** you, the God of **Sinai**, before God, the God of **Israel**. You **sent** abundant rain, O God, to refresh the weary **land**. There your people **finally** settled, and with a bountiful **harvest**, O God, you provided for your **needy** people. The **Lord gives** the **word**, and a **great army brings** the good **news**. **Enemy kings** and **their** armies flee, while the **women** of Israel **divide** the **plunder**. **Even those** who **lived among** the sheepfolds found treasures— **doves** with **wings** of **silver** and feathers of gold. The Almighty scattered the enemy kings like a blowing snowstorm on Mount **Zalmon**. (NLT)

```
F N R I D E L A N D P J O T
L G Z N P X Q N E E D Y U H
M O P N P F T A A V D T T O
F T R L U A R M Y I K R H S
S F P D U H O O V L A E E E
W U O Y I N V I M E Y V I V
E W I N G S D E D L X L R D
N T N E S E R E L Y B I Y K
U A A B J S H A R V E S T Q
E R O E R C N D E N F E C I
V V Z I R I M E E L O V S H
F V E A F G N M V J R O G V
A T M N L B Y G D A E D N H
H B L I I M S R S S E V I G
E X Q S F A O W I R B H K O
I E J E T W R N E M O W B D
```

Solution on Page 362

Even the Dogs Eat Scraps

The Gospel of Mark 7:25–30

Right **away** a **woman** who had heard about him **came** and **fell** at his feet. Her **little** **girl** was possessed by an **evil** **spirit**, and she begged him to **cast** **out** the **demon** **from** her daughter. **Since** she was a **Gentile**, **born** in **Syrian** Phoenicia, **Jesus** **told** her, "First I should **feed** the children—my **own** **family**, the **Jews**. It isn't right to **take** **food** from the children and throw it to the **dogs**." She replied, "That's **true**, **Lord**, but **even** the dogs **under** the **table** are allowed to **eat** the **scraps** from the children's plates." "Good answer!" he **said**. "Now go **home**, for the demon has **left** your daughter." And when she **arrived** home, she found her little girl **lying** quietly in **bed**, and the demon was **gone**. (NLT)

Solution on Page 362

```
V Q D J N Q G I S G W D T J
C G R W W L B A J P E X G N
X S O A J S I Y W E N Q D C
L H L N I D O O F W S H O R
K O S N E V E F G F U U G J
F M C T R U E N A I R Y S T
F E R S E O I O A M F B D P
W C A M E Y B M G M I L E V
M E P R L S L E F T O L B D
C K S I R P V D O T I W Y U
W A D G G I L I T T L E Z L
M T S H L R V H N L U L A S
Q A W T R I W E E N C B Y O
W E C L I T G F D G L A U G
Q N D S G S W E J H W T U M
Q Z J P M O R F P A S V Q A
```

Solution on Page 362

God Blesses Judah

Joel 3:17–21

"So you shall **know** that I am the **LORD your God**, who **dwells** in **Zion**, my **holy mountain**. And Jerusalem shall be holy, and strangers shall **never again pass through** it. And in that **day** the mountains shall **drip sweet wine**, and the **hills** shall **flow** with **milk**, and **all** the streambeds of Judah shall flow with **water**; and a **fountain** shall **come forth from** the **house** of the LORD and water the Valley of **Shittim**. Egypt shall become a desolation and **Edom** a **desolate** wilderness, for the **violence done** to the **people** of Judah, **because** they have **shed innocent blood** in **their land**. But Judah shall be **inhabited** forever, and Jerusalem to all generations. I will **avenge** their blood, blood I have not avenged, for the LORD dwells in Zion." (ESV)

```
M I L K H Q P H O U S E R M
Y K O E T H R O U G H S C N
C E R Q I B W M F B I W D V
C R D L D E S O L A T E A Y
B W L O L C H R O N T E G K
R S O P M A E F W I I T A H
U L O N N U D I B A M Q I T
B E X S K S N A R T J M N R
P H O L Y E H R R N O E E O
V I O L E N C E U U C D V F
W T H E I R G T N O P O E I
J U J W E N J T N F Y N R B
I L Z D E P A N C O M E Y R
O Y J V A I I O V G T N U U
L L A S N R P I L A N D A Y
P Y S G O D T Z W B W J I C
```

Solution on Page 362

Going Home

The Gospel of Mark 6:1–6

Jesus **left** that place and **went** to his hometown. His disciples followed him. When the **day** of worship **came**, he **began** to **teach** in the synagogue. He amazed many who **heard** him. They **asked**, "Where **did** this **man** get these **ideas**? Who **gave** him this **kind** of **wisdom** and the **ability** to do **such** **great** miracles? Isn't this the carpenter, the **son** of Mary, and the brother of **James**, **Joseph**, Judas, and **Simon**? Aren't his **sisters** **here** with us?" So they **took** offense at him. But Jesus **told** them, "The **only** place a **prophet** isn't **honored** is in his hometown, **among** his relatives, and in his **own** house." He couldn't **work** any miracles there **except** to **lay** his **hands** on a **few** **sick** **people** and **cure** them. **Their** unbelief amazed him. (GW)

```
L H O V N C H Z F R M X J C
P E C A V C G C E Q D W L L
F R R A S P R H U F Z L E E
X E E D E H E O S S D H O F
G W K M M T A L R N A P R T
R M D E A O T P E C X E A H
D D R R J C D C T K Y S D E
J R Q U A O J S S T D O R I
V P Q C F E K E I I O J O R
V R S D N A H L S W M A N R
M O A N G A I P N U T O O K
P P R A O B G O V K S N N L
U H V M A S K E D A Y L A A
D E R O N O H P B N D Y A G
D T T N E W O R K S I C K Y
B H P G Y R V U B H D K X V
```

Solution on Page 363

Moses Flees to Midian

Exodus 2:11–15

In the course of time Moses **grew** up. Then he **went** to **see** his **own** **people** and watched them suffering **under** **forced** **labor**. He **saw** a **Hebrew**, **one** of his own people, **being** beaten by an Egyptian. He **looked** **all** around, and when he didn't see anyone, he **beat** the Egyptian to **death** and **hid** the **body** in the sand. When Moses went **there** the **next** **day**, he saw **two** Hebrew **men** fighting. He **asked** the one who started the **fight**, "Why are you beating another Hebrew?" The **man** asked, "Who made you our **ruler** and **judge**? Are you **going** to **kill** me as you killed the Egyptian?" Then Moses was **afraid** and thought that everyone **knew** **what** he had done. When **Pharaoh** **heard** what Moses had done, he **tried** to have him killed. But Moses **fled** **from** Pharaoh and settled in the **land** of **Midian**. (GW)

```
N R O W N D A N G Y O P O L
B F R W E S M S R X I A W J
E N F A M L L I K W H A T Z
W H T F O R C E D E K O O L
H H O R A A R L A I D E L F
V H M A Z M O R F D A G W R
O T I I R D D N O N E N A N
W F W D B A B G T H G I F E
Q Q L Q W Y H K S D D E R X
M J F A E E H P S M U B Y T
T O S T B T N T E O J M A N
O O W R A O S K G O I N G E
H L E E Y E R E H T P L H W
F W A D R O B E E R U L E R
W J O N W G Y B J H H A E L
P B F U D V J T T W E X E Q
```

Solution on Page 363

Test of Faith

James 1:2–7

My **brothers** and **sisters**, be very **happy** when you are **tested** in different **ways**. You **know** that **such** testing of **your** **faith** produces endurance. **Endure** **until** your testing is **over**. Then you will be **mature** and **complete**, and you won't **need** anything. If any of you needs **wisdom** to know **what** you **should** do, you should **ask** **God**, and he will **give** it to you. God is generous to everyone and doesn't **find** **fault** with them. When you ask for something, don't have any **doubts**. A **person** who has doubts is like a **wave** that is **blown** by the **wind** and tossed by the **sea**. A person who has doubts shouldn't **expect** to **receive** anything **from** the **Lord**. A person who has doubts is thinking **about** **two** different **things** at the **same** **time** and can't **make** up his **mind** about anything. (GW)

```
F I K X H U S Q R U O Y U B
T V Y C A K Y K M V F R O M
D O U B T S A N E A H Y V C
R S O G R A W R U U W D O M
R U S V O O U L E Q N M A A
T Z K G L D T H L I P T J K
W P R B N N T H F L U E I E
E Y E E V I E C E R Y S N L
H V M R A N H T E R G T N O
Y Y A F S R E T S I S E O R
W I S W O O C W V H E D A D
A S I D L E N E O D F N W T
S R Y P P A H U E N M I I A
S S P X Q T L T B P K M N H
I V E M O D S I W K E W D W
J U X A A H L S U O J H P P
```

Solution on Page 363

The Lord Reigns Forever

Psalms 9:1–9

I will **praise** you, **LORD**, with **all** my **heart**; I will **tell** of all the marvelous **things** you have **done**. I will be **filled** with **joy because** of you. I will **sing** praises to **your name**, O **Most High**. My enemies retreated; they staggered and **died** when you **appeared**. For you have judged in my **favor**; **from** your **throne** you have judged with **fairness**. You have **rebuked** the **nations** and destroyed the **wicked**; you have **erased their** names **forever**. The **enemy** is finished, in **endless ruins**; the **cities** you uprooted are now forgotten. But the LORD **reigns** forever, executing judgment from his throne. He will **judge** the **world** with **justice** and **rule** the nations with fairness. The LORD is a **shelter** for the oppressed, a **refuge** in **times** of **trouble**. (NLT)

```
Q W S Y S F Y Y T H E I R T
R D D E K C I W C E N E M Y
D W L O M N N L E I I R O O
M O R F N I A Y L G T U S J
W D O N E E T M N E R I T D
D V W D T B S S E L D N E R
L I R E F O R E V E R S E S
L C E G S S E N R I A F I P
E T R D M B L A R R U N T R
T R O U B L E E E G G Z H A
M A V J A P T C E J E L I I
V E A I P L V N A T I O N S
B H F A E C I T S U J R G E
S G T H R O N E S G S D S V
X I S E L U R E B U K E D P
I H O B J U G J H E K D F L
```

Solution on Page 363

Forty Days and Forty Nights

Genesis 7:1–5

And **Jehovah** **said** **unto** **Noah**, **Come** thou and **all** **thy** house **into** the **ark**; for thee have I seen **righteous** before me in this **generation**. Of **every** **clean** **beast** thou shalt **take** to thee seven and seven, the male and his female; and of the beasts that are not clean **two**, the male and his female: of the **birds** also of the **heavens**, seven and seven, male and female, to **keep** **seed** alive **upon** the **face** of all the earth. For yet seven **days**, and I will **cause** it to **rain** upon the earth **forty** days and forty **nights**; and every **living** thing that I have **made** will I **destroy** **from** **off** the face of the **ground**. And Noah **did** according unto all that Jehovah commanded him. (ASV)

```
U E A H V O C J A W X V O T
P G G Z P G F F O L C P A S
O R T N X K E A S C L K L G
N N D T Y T O C Q T E D I N
C I F X Q W H E S U A C G O
D I G I T H Y A Q A N K N I
E B I H K Z E O V E I O I T
T V F E T B Y T R O F D V A
S V E U I S U O E T H G I R
Q P S R H E A V E N S E L E
T D D H Y R L T D E M E J N
E S O A K I F V E I C O D E
V O J O Y X J D D N U O R G
X O T N U S S L A T I I M F
W T G Q I Z G N M O Q A E E
B A V B V Y A J M L V G R F
```

Solution on Page 364

Know the Truth

1 John 2:20–25

But ye have an unction **from** the **Holy One**, and ye **know all things**. I have not **written unto** you **because** ye know not the **truth**, but because ye know it, and that no **lie** is of the truth. Who is a liar but he that **denieth** that **Jesus** is the **Christ**? He is antichrist, that denieth the **Father** and the Son. Whosoever denieth the Son, the **same hath** not the Father: he that acknowledgeth the Son hath the Father also. Let that **therefore abide** in you, **which** ye have **heard** from the **beginning**. If that which ye have heard from the beginning shall **remain** in you, ye also shall continue in the Son, and in the Father. And this is the **promise** that he hath promised us, **even** eternal life. (KJV)

Solution on Page 354

```
H O F B K U J C B A Z R S F
F E R O F E R E H T B H U L
U T F W N R G S A B I D E C
N Q W O C I V U I M E V E N
P P U R N J H A M N S M M E
C O M N I E J C I C U B E Z
O T I K L T E E A H S S V L
S N D Y O V T B S R E I H Y
G U H W Q H N E E I J A I W
N E Q M F Q N P N S M Z R W
I Y X X D U T I H T Z O G D
H C I H W H E F A T H E R E
T H Z O S W R I L M A O I P
M P O J A O C C L O E H L G
C P H K M N H L H T U R T Y
A A T Z E K D A Q W X Q X P
```

Solution on Page 364

Beware False Wisdom

Colossians 2:18–23

Let no **one** disqualify you, insisting on asceticism and worship of **angels**, going on in **detail** **about** visions, **puffed** up **without** reason by his **sensuous** **mind**, and not **holding** **fast** to the **Head**, **from** **whom** the whole **body**, nourished and **knit** together **through** its **joints** and **ligaments**, **grows** with a growth that is from **God**. If with **Christ** you **died** to the elemental **spirits** of the **world**, why, as if you were **still** alive in the world, do you **submit** to regulations—"Do not **handle**, Do not **taste**, Do not **touch**" (referring to **things** that **all** **perish** as they are used)—according to **human** **precepts** and teachings? **These** have **indeed** an appearance of **wisdom** in promoting self-made religion and asceticism and **severity** to the body, but they are of no value in **stopping** the indulgence of the **flesh**. (ESV)

```
X N P W I S D O M S U S M B
F A S T G S G Q U H C U O T
R M G N I P P O T S H A H H
O U I C Q D U I V P R G W G
M H F L E S H V R L I R Y U
T I N K N T A E S I S O M O
H F G E S N C U U A T W S R
E L S T G E B D D T D S J H
S S I E P M V E M E I Q O T
E L L T I A Q E O D E L U P
L S S T B G X D R J D O H D
O L B T O I B N O I H C E L
M H A N D L E I N T T F A R
B F E I Y O N G I F F Y D O
B E T S A T G W T U O B A W
O B A H S I R E P M I N D L
```

Solution on Page 364

The Lord Is Good

Lamentations 3:24–33

The **LORD** is my **portion**, **saith** my **soul**; therefore will I **hope** in him. The LORD is **good unto** them that **wait** for him, to the soul that **seeketh** him. It is good that a **man should both** hope and **quietly** wait for the salvation of the LORD. It is good for a man that he **bear** the **yoke** in his **youth**. He sitteth **alone** and **keepeth silence**, because he **hath borne** it **upon** him. He **putteth** his **mouth** in the **dust**; if so be **there** may be hope. He **giveth** his **cheek** to him that smiteth him: he is **filled full** with reproach. For the LORD will not **cast off** for **ever**: But **though** he **cause grief**, yet will he have compassion according to the multitude of his mercies. For he **doth** not **afflict** willingly **nor** grieve the children of **men**. (KJV)

```
Q S V M J J J V Y Y J I C G U
Q Z W C J R Y H R E V E P N
A L U O S H O U L D R O O T
S Z E S I L E N C E N R O B
K C H T E V I G H L C A L I
P M C H E E K T P L H L M E
Q O B K B W K J O I U T H P
Z U N T O Y F E R F G Y A O
J T I K E E P E T H O U G H
D H G E S U A C I H O T F T
U A R T T E I U O T D S R U
S A I T H L M E N O L A N O
T K E F F T Y L W B E C F Y
C T F F I L O C S B C K F K
H W A A P R K D N C U F O V
A F W Z D H Y C H G E G O Y
```

Solution on Page 364

Count the Stars

Genesis 15:2–7

Abram asked, "Almighty **LORD**, **what** will you **give** me? **Since** I'm **going** to **die** without **children**, **Eliezer** of Damascus will **inherit** my household. You have given me no children, so this **member** of my household will be my **heir**." **Suddenly**, the LORD **spoke** his **word** to Abram **again**. He **said**, "This **man** will not be your heir. Your **own son** will be your heir." He **took** Abram outside and said, "Now **look** up at the **sky** and count the **stars**, if you are **able** to count them." He also said to him, "That's how many descendants you will have!" Then Abram **believed** the LORD, and the LORD **regarded** that **faith** to be his **approval** of Abram. Then the LORD said to him, "I am the LORD, who brought you **out** of Ur." (GW)

Solution on Page 364

```
M Z C G X O H I I C E Y O S
L R R L M H Z E D T J Q D O
P E K W D U D I I V S O N S
G G H E L I E Z E R I F N O
L A P P R O V A L B N J K M
T R C I N H E R I T C W V D
J D S L C H I L D R E N O W
U E D S R Y L N E D D U S X
V D F L G E E V A P R P J I
J N Y G S S B Q K O O T C E
J I M N A T U M J K W X J I
T K N I A G A W E L B A A X
W A D O E R I R J M O B L W
M W W G B O O V S K Y O U T
U T F A I T H P E W R W K C
K B N S O E Y R U D R F B D
```

Solution on Page 365

Offerings

Leviticus 3:12–16

"If his offering is a **goat**, then he shall **offer** it **before** the LORD and **lay** his **hand** on its **head** and **kill** it in front of the **tent** of **meeting**, and the **sons** of **Aaron** shall **throw** its **blood against** the **sides** of the altar. Then he shall offer **from** it, as his offering for a **food** offering to the LORD, the **fat covering** the **entrails** and **all** the fat that is on the entrails and the **two kidneys** with the fat that is on them at the **loins** and the **long lobe** of the **liver** that he shall remove with the kidneys. And the **priest** shall **burn** them on the altar as a food offering with a **pleasing** aroma. All fat is the LORD's." (ESV)

Solution on Page 365

```
N T B V G P G Y I Y Z K H V
Y E E N G U F Q B T E K X R
B N X F J G D T S E I R P W
M T Q B U R N T M D B G Q O
L A Y L A G A I N S T O L L
P O C Q M I H E R H K L L O
D G V S S E Y P R E L I G I
V O N L D S E O N A V F L Y
G O H I S S W T U D L O B L
S Y S F S S R O I I I L C B
J T E E G A R B I N O E N R
B Y D H I O E U S O G N O L
M N I L F F V L D R W M W V
J F S R O F I K P A R Q T E
P G O R O E L U T A F T J Y
N M E D D R M K D C N R O O
```

Solution on Page 365

Peter Resurrects Tabitha

Acts 9:36–40

Now there was in **Joppa** a disciple named Tabitha, **which**, translated, means **Dorcas**. She was **full** of **good** **works** and **acts** of charity. In **those** **days** she became **ill** and **died**, and when they had washed her, they **laid** her in an **upper** **room**. **Since** **Lydda** was **near** Joppa, the disciples, hearing that **Peter** was there, **sent** **two** **men** to him, **urging** him, "**Please** come to us without **delay**." So Peter **rose** and **went** with them. And when he arrived, they **took** him to the upper room. **All** the widows stood **beside** him weeping and showing **tunics** and **other** garments that Dorcas **made** while she was with them. But Peter put them all outside, and **knelt** **down** and **prayed**; and turning to the **body** he said, "Tabitha, **arise**." And she **opened** her **eyes**, and when she saw Peter she **sat** up. (ESV)

```
J C F Q N A P W K D P T R W
N T T Y B E S E N T E L H S
T B N O T E S A E L P I K A
R M D E Y A R P L G C R D T
E Y R H C A H H T H O S E H
K J R R P Y D S R W D X Z L
N A O P E N E D E L A Y L R
E D I S E B O S Y Y D A Y S
A O S C R O O M I L E I T C
R W G I G H U R T R L C Y F
O N F N N Q P E G L A I D A
S T B U I C P H D P A L I K
E A W T L G E T P A O M N X
N O N O S L R O V K M F N V
W E V O W S J U N Z T C W T
W V M K Z Q N I T R T B A U
```

Solution on Page 365

Jesus Is Buried

The Gospel of Luke 23:50–56

Now there was a **man named Joseph**, **from** the **Jewish town** of Arimathea. He was a **member** of the **council**, a **good** and **righteous** man, who had not consented to **their** decision and action; and he was **looking** for the **kingdom** of God. This man **went** to **Pilate** and **asked** for the **body** of Jesus. Then he **took** it **down** and **wrapped** it in a **linen shroud** and laid him in a **tomb cut** in stone, where no **one** had **ever** yet been laid. It was the **day** of Preparation, and the Sabbath was beginning. The women who had **come** with him from **Galilee followed** and **saw** the tomb and how his body was laid. Then they **returned** and prepared **spices** and **ointments**. On the Sabbath they rested according to the commandment. (ESV)

```
V K H Z V H H A C N F Z G U
M Q Z T J O S E P H R M N Z
I D O W N E N I L G O A W J
E M R R X D F J W D M N O Y
B E E L I L A G X E E J T F
S Y V W A G P Y D W J K A T
D W F E Y W H I S O L G S E
K R Z N R I W T V L I O N A
K X E T R R N A E L C O M E
K O I B A E A Z S O N D Y W
I I I O P M Z T E S F U D T A
N M P T R E T U C E O S J O
G E N Y H A M Z R B C F L Z
D I T B L O O K I N G I F F
O L R I E H T A G V E A P R
M G P O Q Y S H R O U D D S
```

Solution on Page 365

The Desires of the Righteous

Proverbs 10:21–28

The **lips** of the righteous **feed** many, but fools **die** for **lack** of sense. The **blessing** of the **LORD** makes **rich**, and he **adds** no **sorrow** with it. **Doing wrong** is like a joke to a **fool**, but **wisdom** is **pleasure** to a **man** of understanding. **What** the **wicked dreads** will **come upon** him, but the **desire** of the righteous will be **granted**. When the **tempest passes**, the wicked is no more, but the righteous is established **forever**. Like **vinegar** to the **teeth** and **smoke** to the **eyes**, so is the sluggard to **those** who **send** him. The **fear** of the LORD **prolongs life**, but the **years** of the wicked will be **short**. The **hope** of the righteous **brings joy**, but the expectation of the wicked will **perish**. (ESV)

```
P S H O R T H O S E Y E S G
E I D F M G N S S J P L N O
V H N A J N N O E P O H W L
T P N D E O R I S S H Y P O
L C R K N R T D S T S V P R
Q O O O O W D E E S I A G T
L M O W L A E E M N E Z P A
S E H F V O T Y E P D L D H
T W S B D E N G E O E E B W
D X I G N O A G I A S S I M
F N R S N R R N S I R C T N
F E E D D I G U R F K S O L
U X P S F O R E V E R P R A
V P L I F E M B D C U I I M
R W B D I L A C K Q C L Y Z
D G E A V U R R Q H Z I A H
```

Solution on Page 366

The Value of Knowing Christ

Philippians 3:7–11

I once **thought these things** were valuable, but now I consider them **worthless because** of **what Christ** has done. **Yes**, everything **else** is worthless when **compared** with the **infinite** value of knowing Christ **Jesus** my **Lord**. For his **sake** I have **discarded** everything else, counting it **all** as **garbage**, so that I **could gain** Christ and **become one** with him. I no longer count on my **own** righteousness **through obeying** the **law**; rather, I become righteous through **faith** in Christ. For God's **way** of **making** us **right** with **himself depends** on faith. I want to know Christ and **experience** the **mighty** power that **raised** him **from** the **dead**. I want to **suffer** with him, **sharing** in his death, so that one way or another I will experience the resurrection from the dead! (NLT)

```
T R E F F U S W E S E H T K
H D E P T H R O U G H T M X
G V E S S H A R I N G N W T
U N E S U U C T S I R H C I
O R I Z I A E H O H A S F O
H E I Y J A C L M T D D W W
T E C N E I R E P X E N P M
U G I M F B U S B D R E L D
N A S R L I O S R R A P O S
G B E I E W N A L L P E R A
W R X G S M C I G C M D D K
L A W H M S O A T A O S D E
F G H T I A F C K E C U L D
L R F D H P W I E D Y S L D
S N O Z R J N A L B E E A D
S D P M I G H T Y A J J S U
```

Solution on Page 366

The Messenger

Malachi 3:1–4

"Behold, I **send** my messenger, and he will **prepare** the **way before** me. And the **Lord whom** you **seek** will **suddenly come** to his **temple**; and the messenger of the **covenant** in whom you **delight**, behold, he is coming, **says** the LORD of **hosts**. But who **can endure** the **day** of his coming, and who can **stand** when he **appears**? For he is like a refiner's **fire** and like fullers' **soap**. He will **sit** as a refiner and purifier of silver, and he will **purify** the **sons** of **Levi** and **refine** them like gold and silver, and they will **bring** offerings in righteousness to the LORD. Then the **offering** of Judah and **Jerusalem** will be pleasing to the LORD as in the days of **old** and as in **former years**." (ESV)

Solution on Page 356

```
N B H U Y S A B Y A W T W V
H C T Z E Q Y D N A T S A J
M H O E M X I P S S D T O Y
Y U K E R O V V B R S S L I
P X F F K A H R E M R O F M
J C O C D K P F F L R H A W
N J E W E S I E O D U T N P
Q E E U H N M M R K A G I J
O O Y R E O U O E P V N D S
P X F H U S M C P U R I F Y
X Y F F N S E E Y E A R S A
P C O V E N A N T D I B V S
B A M R D R Y L N E D D U S
Z N I U S R I E E L P M E T
Y F R Q E R S N O M T Y T S
U E U R N G T H G I L E D M
```

Solution on Page 366

Follow Me

The Gospel of Luke 9:57–62

As they were **going** along the **road**, someone said to him, "I will follow you **wherever** you go." And **Jesus** said to him, "Foxes have **holes**, and **birds** of the **air** have **nests**, but the Son of **Man** has nowhere to **lay** his head." To another he said, "Follow me." But he said, "**Lord**, let me first go and **bury** my father." And Jesus said to him, "Leave the **dead** to bury **their own** dead. But as for you, go and proclaim the **kingdom** of God." Yet another said, "I will follow you, Lord, but let me first **say farewell** to **those** at my home." Jesus said to him, "No **one** who **puts** his **hand** to the plow and **looks back** is **fit** for the kingdom of God." (ESV)

```
M D Q G D E Z W V W N Y H R
J E S U S Y H T Y K F A Z N
L A M O D E N P J F H G H Q
L D H W R M L N L X O T F B
E T Q E I O L O G B L Y J Y
W M V M B D R O H A B O K V
E E O S A D I W O C U J S C
R Y A D W N T N O K S T U P
A V Q O G Q H N U B S A Y A
F I T Q E N E Y D E U U W G
S F B X N Y I Y N A J Y A B
I Y R Z A O R K A C O V G X
Y Z N R U Y I U H L J R G N
Q P M O D G A L B L L C K P
W U D P P W O N R H D S T F
I B T K S L Z R M U T T G I
```

Solution on Page 366

Be Faithful

Malachi 2:13–16

And this second **thing** you do. You **cover** the **LORD**'s **altar** with **tears**, with **weeping** and **groaning because** he no longer **regards** the **offering** or **accepts** it with **favor from your hand**. But you **say**, "Why does he not?" Because the LORD was **witness between** you and the **wife** of your youth, to **whom** you have been **faithless**, **though** she is your companion and your wife by covenant. **Did** he not make them **one**, with a portion of the **Spirit** in **their** union? And **what** was the one **God seeking**? Godly **offspring**. So **guard** yourselves in your spirit, and let none of you be faithless to the wife of your youth. "For the **man** who does not **love** his wife but divorces her, says the LORD, the God of **Israel**, covers his **garment** with **violence**, says the LORD of **hosts**. So guard yourselves in your spirit, and do not be faithless." (ESV)

```
F R T E N O I I W X T N G G
Z I S R A E L W H R U N A G
U E G D H O E E A S I R N P
A H N I R V S W T H M I Y B
H T I D O U S P T E K A W W
B D P L A A E C N E L O I V
H V E C Y C L T E T B F T X
G F E Q C T H S A V E G N X
U B W A S F T R D P N R E W
O F F S P R I N G I E P S N
H Y G N I N A O R G A P S F
T F A M P H F E A E I L C V
G U A R D K F R T R V F M L
B N U V H F D U I N R O K L
G O D T O S S T S O H N C V
Y G K Z Y R S Z M W S E A Y
```

Solution on Page 367

Holy Conduct

1 Peter 1:13–19

Therefore, preparing **your minds** for action, and being sober-minded, **set** your **hope fully** on the **grace** that will be **brought** to you at the **revelation** of **Jesus Christ**. As **obedient** children, do not be conformed to the passions of your **former** ignorance, but as he who called you is **holy**, you also be holy in **all** your **conduct**, since it is written, "You shall be holy, for I am holy." And if you call on him as **Father** who judges impartially **according** to **each** one's **deeds**, conduct yourselves with **fear throughout** the **time** of your exile, knowing that you were **ransomed from** the **futile ways inherited** from your forefathers, not with **perishable things such** as **silver** or gold, but with the **precious blood** of Christ, like that of a lamb without **blemish** or spot. (ESV)

```
S J C Y R J H K G H C A E B
R G X R F M F A T H E R L M
E U N F O R M E R L D E G D
V P O I S D N I M O M K F C
L Q O Y H K S U O I C E R P
I U W H E T S L S Y L L O E
S N C N W I B H H B L R M M
A U H R E V E L A T I O N I
S C Z E T U O H G U O R H T
O O C G R W S B B N F A W H
H N J O J I L F E G U E S G
R D Z E R B T S U D T F A U
N U T E S D S E D L I L G O
X C P D K U I Y D E L E J R
Y T D E M O S N A R E Y N B
V V X F E C A R G W M D K T
```

Solution on Page 367

Your Father Knows What You Need

The Gospel of Matthew 6:6–13

"But when you **pray**, go **into** **your** **room** and **shut** the **door** and pray to your Father who is in **secret**. And your Father who **sees** in secret will **reward** you. And when you pray, do not **heap** up **empty** phrases as the **Gentiles** do, for they **think** that they will be heard for **their** **many** **words**. Do not be like them, for your Father **knows** **what** you **need** **before** you **ask** him. Pray then like this: Our Father in heaven, **hallowed** be your **name**. Your **kingdom** **come**, your will be **done**, on **earth** as it is in heaven. **Give** us this **day** our daily **bread**, and forgive us our **debts**, as we **also** have forgiven our debtors. And **lead** us not into temptation, but **deliver** us **from** **evil**." (ESV)

```
R I F G X R Y A K G A C C Y
I M P T C O K N O W S D Z I
C O M E U D E R O F E B T S
Y R D R A W E R T W L N H N
V F M C P R F L O K I U G E
J F J E D E I L I Y T P M E
E B A S K V L N V V N D M D
X K A D E A G E B R E A D L
B W W P H D J H A B G R M O
Z H O T O H Y L T D I I A S
V O R M S Q U S H E A P V E
X A D D L K N I H T M J Y E
E Y S O A B N T A H W A M S
Y I A O N T G X K A D J N J
M O O R O E Z X O E P J K N
R X X S P W R A N R K U W F
```

Solution on Page 367

Meat and Bread

Exodus 16:11–15

And the **LORD** said to **Moses**, "I have heard the **grumbling** of the **people** of **Israel**. Say to them, 'At **twilight** you **shall** **eat** meat, and in the **morning** you shall be **filled** with bread. Then you shall **know** that I am the LORD **your** God.'" In the **evening** **quail** **came** up and **covered** the camp, and in the morning **dew** **lay** **around** the camp. And when the dew had gone up, **there** was on the **face** of the wilderness a **fine**, flake-like **thing**, fine as **frost** on the **ground**. When the people of Israel **saw** it, they said to **one** another, "**What** is it?" For they **did** not know what it was. And Moses said to them, "It is the bread that the LORD has **given** you to eat." (ESV)

Solution on Page 357

```
W L E I F M J O V N R Q D Y
S A E Y M Q Z N G R C F V N
J Y S A O V W E D Q H S M I
M A L T R U U C U X P W L E
D R E H N S R A G Y O H I Z
C D R G I S I F I N E S B U
F Q E I N L Z F K F U I H U
W Q H L G I L A Z V A R G L
F H T I L I L A R T O E R Z
E E A W M I V B H O H Z O X
T M L T T T F E M S U I U J
Z A A P S L O I N U F N N E
K C E E O M C O V E R E D G
P I S R R E V E N I N G I N
I O D B F D P M Q G A T D V
M I Z L E J H Y N O X W L A
```

Solution on Page 367

Answers

327

Our Many Sins

I Will Free You

**Servant and Master
Are Equal**

Deny Yourself

328

Believe in the Light

Jesus' Authority Is Challenged

Watch for Divisions

The Merchants Will Weep

Miracles and Healings

The Burning Bush

Mount Sinai

The Trumpets

A Good Name

Sit in the Lowest Place

God Makes a Promise

A Lamb for His Offering

One Died for All

As for Me and My House

Paul and Silas in Prison

A Feast to the Lord

The Importance of Wisdom and Understanding

Jesus Clears the Temple

A Paralyzed Man Is Forgiven

Love One Another

What God Has Done

Go and Bring Forth Fruit

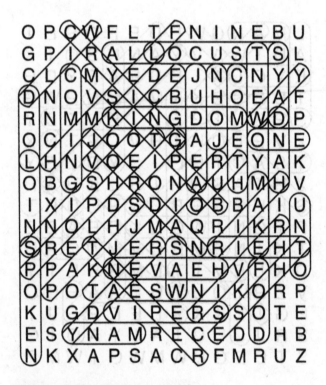

The Kingdom of Heaven Is At Hand

Fools and the Wise

Win Her Back

Ten Lepers

The True Light

Jesus Performs Miracles

The Wrath of God Against Ungodliness

The Ark and Dagon

The Righteous Escape

Do Not Cause a Brother to Fall

I Will Give You Rest

The First-Born

A Foolish Son

I Have Taken Refuge in You

Warning to the Rich

Ruth Marries Boaz

Cherish Wisdom

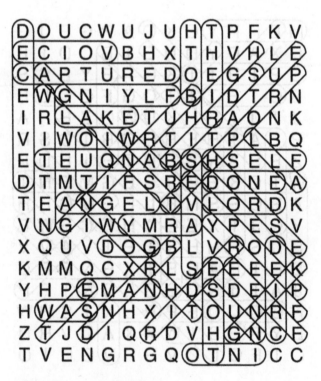

King of Kings

Take a Lesson from the Ants

Love Your Enemies

Love the Lord Your God

Children Through Faith

The Church Grows

The Power of Sin Is Broken

A Throne Set in Heaven

Jesus Sends the Twelve

340

Even the Sea Obeys Him

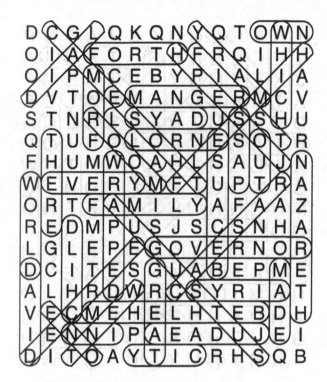

Trip to Bethlehem

Spreading the Good News

A Temple of God

Paul Shook the Dust

Water from the Rock

Abide in Me

Costly Ointment

342

An Angel Appears

The New Heaven and Earth

The Star

Hailstorm

Remain Steadfast

Love God and Your Neighbor

Striving after Wind

True Riches

344

A Lame Man Walks

The Son Is Heir

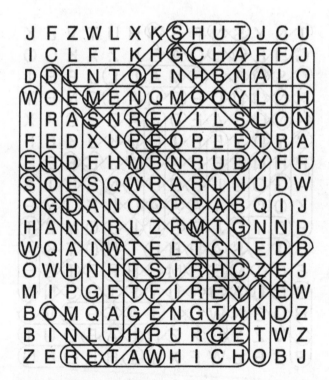

One Mightier Than I Cometh

Make Me to Know Your Ways

She Was Praying

Advice

Many Rooms

Crowds Follow Jesus

346

Living Stone

On a White Horse

Pay Attention!

The Four Chariots

Commanded to Love

Faith Comes from Hearing

Imperishable Beauty

Show the Truth by Action

Speak Wisely

A Faithful Centurion

Daniel in the Lions' Den

You Must Be Born Again

Creation Waits

Faith More
Precious Than Gold

Peter Speaks

The Good Shepherd

350

Dreams and Visions

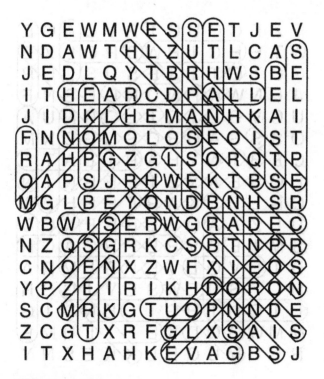

God Gives Solomon Wisdom

The Lord Heals the Brokenhearted

Spiritual Devotion

Fight the Good Fight

Swing Your Sickle Now

A Roman Citizen

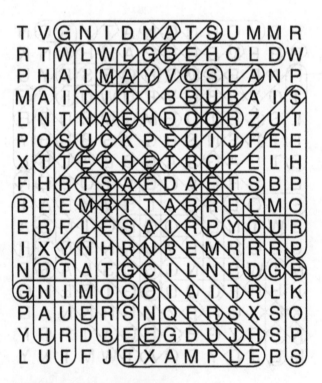

Compassionate and Merciful

Jesus Cried Out

Clothed in White Robes

We Honor the Lord

Prince of Peace

Smooth Talk

Fed with Milk

Flesh and Blood

Job Did Not Sin

I Received Mercy

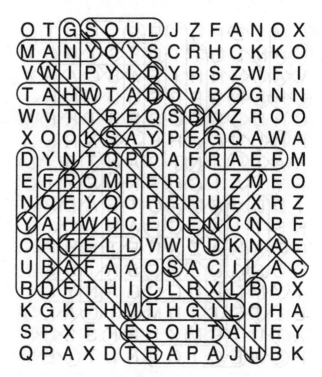

Have No Fear

Don't Leave Me

The Fringe of His Garment

Jesus Expels a Demon

The Lamb Breaks the Seventh Seal

The Man Born Blind

Joyful Song

356

Jacob Wrestles

He Chose Us

Jesus Is Lord of
the Sabbath

The Sixth Seal

Always Seek His Presence

The Hands of Compassionate Women

In the Beginning

Taxes to Caesar

Faith the Size of a Mustard Seed

Consider the Lilies

God Is a Rock

A House on Solid Rock

The Day of the Lord

A Fresh Olive Leaf

The Scroll

Heirs with Christ

God Blessed the Seventh Day

A Good Soldier of Christ Jesus

God Tells Noah of the Flood

Teach Us to Number Our Days

Truly God Has Listened

You Sent Abundant Rain

Even the Dogs Eat Scraps

God Blesses Judah

362

Going Home

Test of Faith

Moses Flees to Midian

The Lord Reigns Forever

Forty Days and Forty Nights

Know the Truth

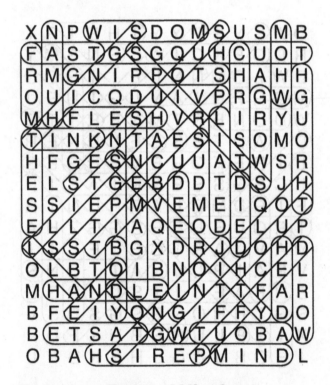

Beware False Wisdom

The Lord Is Good

MZCGXOHIICEYOS
LRRLMHZEDTJQDO
PEKWDUDIIVSONS
GGHELIEZERIFNO
LAPPROVALBNJKM
TRCINHERITCWVD
JDSLCHILDRENOW
UEDSRYLNEDDUSX
VDFLGEEVAPRPJI
JNYGSSBQKOOTCE
JIMNATUMJKWJI
TKNIAGAWELBAAX
WADOERIRJMOBLW
MWWGBOOVSKYOUT
UTFAITHPEWRWKC
KBNSOEYRUDRFBD

Count the Stars

NTBVGPGYIYZKHV
YEENGUFQBTEKXR
BNXFJGDTSEIRPW
MTQBURNTMDBGQO
LAYLAGAINSTOLL
POCQMIHERHKLLO
DGVSSEYPRELIGI
VONLDSEONAVFLY
GOHISSWTUDLOBL
SYSFSSROIIILCB
JTEEGARBINOENR
BYDHIOEUSOGNOL
MNILFFVLDRWMWV
JFSROFIKPARQTE
PGOROELUTAFTJY
NMEDDRMKDCNROO

Offerings

JCFQNAPWKDPTRW
NTTYBESENTELHS
TBNOTESAELPIKA
RMDEYARPLGCRDT
EYRHCAHHTHOSEH
KJRRPYDSRWDXZL
NAOPENEDELAYLR
EDISEBOSYYDAYS
AOSCROOMILEITC
RWGIGHURTRLCYF
ONFNNQPEGLAIDA
STBUICPHDPALIK
EAWTLGETPAOMNX
NONOSLROVKMFNV
WEVOWSJUNZTCWT
WVMKZQNITRTBAU

Peter Resurrects Tabitha

VKHZVHHACNFZGU
MQZTJOSEPHRMNZ
IDOWNENILGOAWJ
EMRRXDFJWDMNOY
BEELILAGXEEJTF
SYVWAGPYDWJKAT
DWFEYWHISOLGSE
KRZNRIWTVLIONA
KXETRRNAELCOME
KOIBAEAZSONDYW
IIOPMZTESFUDTA
NMPTRETUCEOSJO
GENYHAMZRBCFLZ
DITBLOOKINGIFF
OLRIEHTAGVEAPR
MGPOQYSHROUDDS

Jesus Is Buried

The Desires of the Righteous

The Value of Knowing Christ

The Messenger

Follow Me

Be Faithful

Holy Conduct

Your Father Knows What You Need

Meat and Bread

160
SUPERSIZED
PUZZLES!

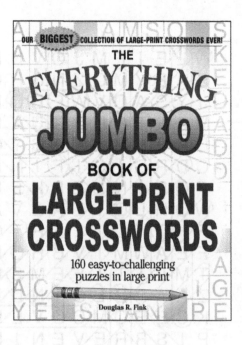
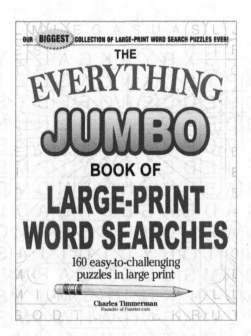